The works of

# Shuna Anderson

## Presented by
## Mark Turner

ISBN 9798871250235

Published by Mark Turner. 55 Wallace Crescent. Roslin. EH25 9LN.
Email: mark@scottishartists.uk  www.scottishartists.uk

# Introduction

I am delighted to present the work of Shuna Anderson who has been painting since childhood, and attended a Fine Art foundation course at Leith School of Art. She describes her work as "Figurative and abstract paintings" and uses mixed media including acrylic paint and charcoal.

The photographs were taken in her flat, and the words attached to each picture are her own.

I find the work would be well suited to family cafe or hotel environments as it tends to be bright and illustrative, and would be equally well suited to be hung as decorations in office space. They would of course be lovely in the home too.

All the work in this book are still for sale as at Dec 2023, and they will be posted on the website until sold.

Shuna has exhibited her work in galleries in France, UK, and Scotland.

# Index to Pictures

# Shuna Anderson

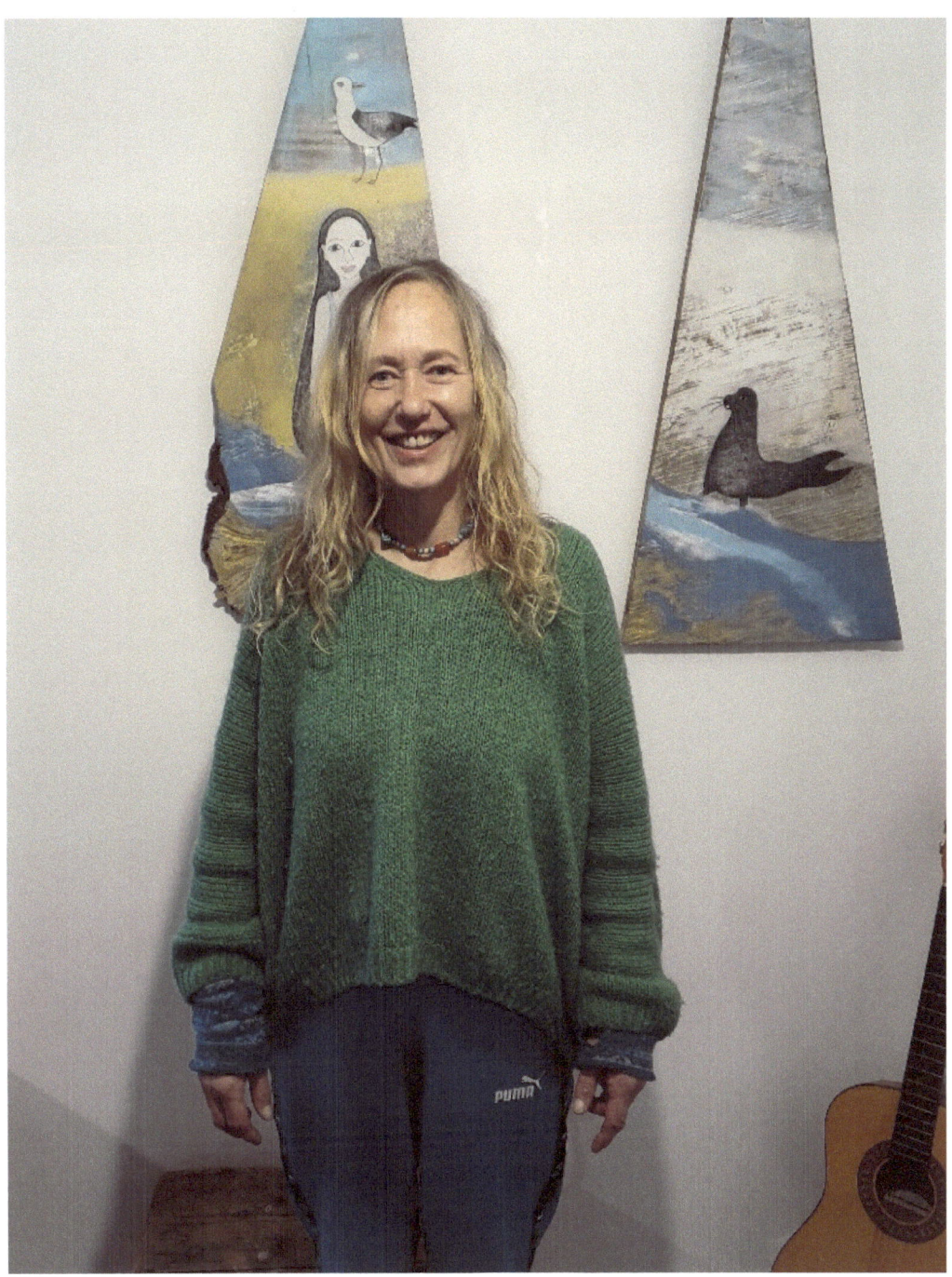

I am delighted to have my work published as part of the "Mark Turner presents" series. This book contains photos of most of the work remaining in my flat which is still for sale as of December 2023.

# Reindeer looking Right

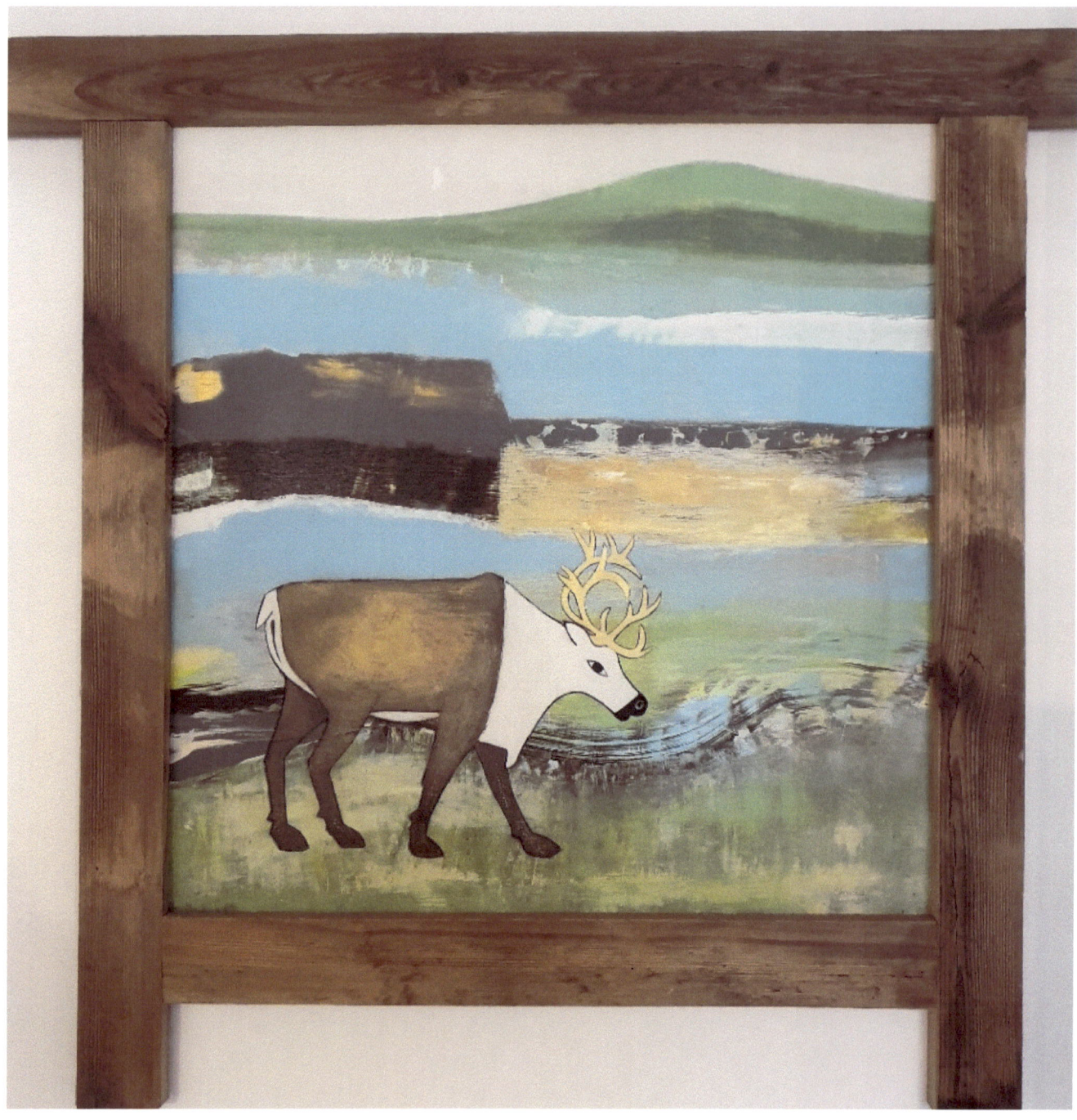

The reindeer is the goddess of wisdom and teaches you to survive, endure, and thrive in the harshest of winters.

The reindeer spirit animal inspires your inner compass to keep your mind clear and your focus sure.

# Reindeer looking Left

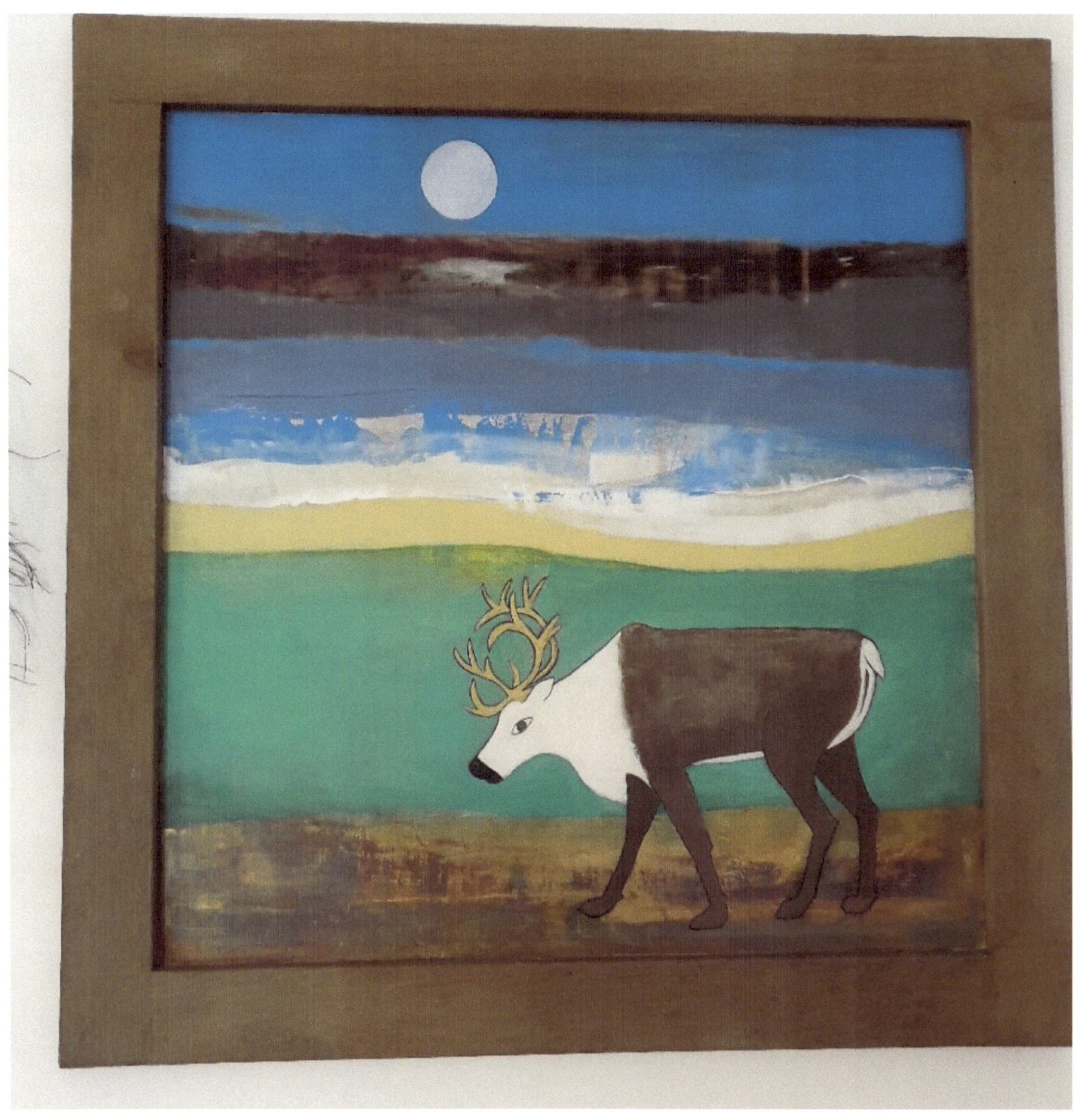

The reindeer symbolism and meaning is to inspire,
motivate and enlighten.

# Blonde Highland Coo

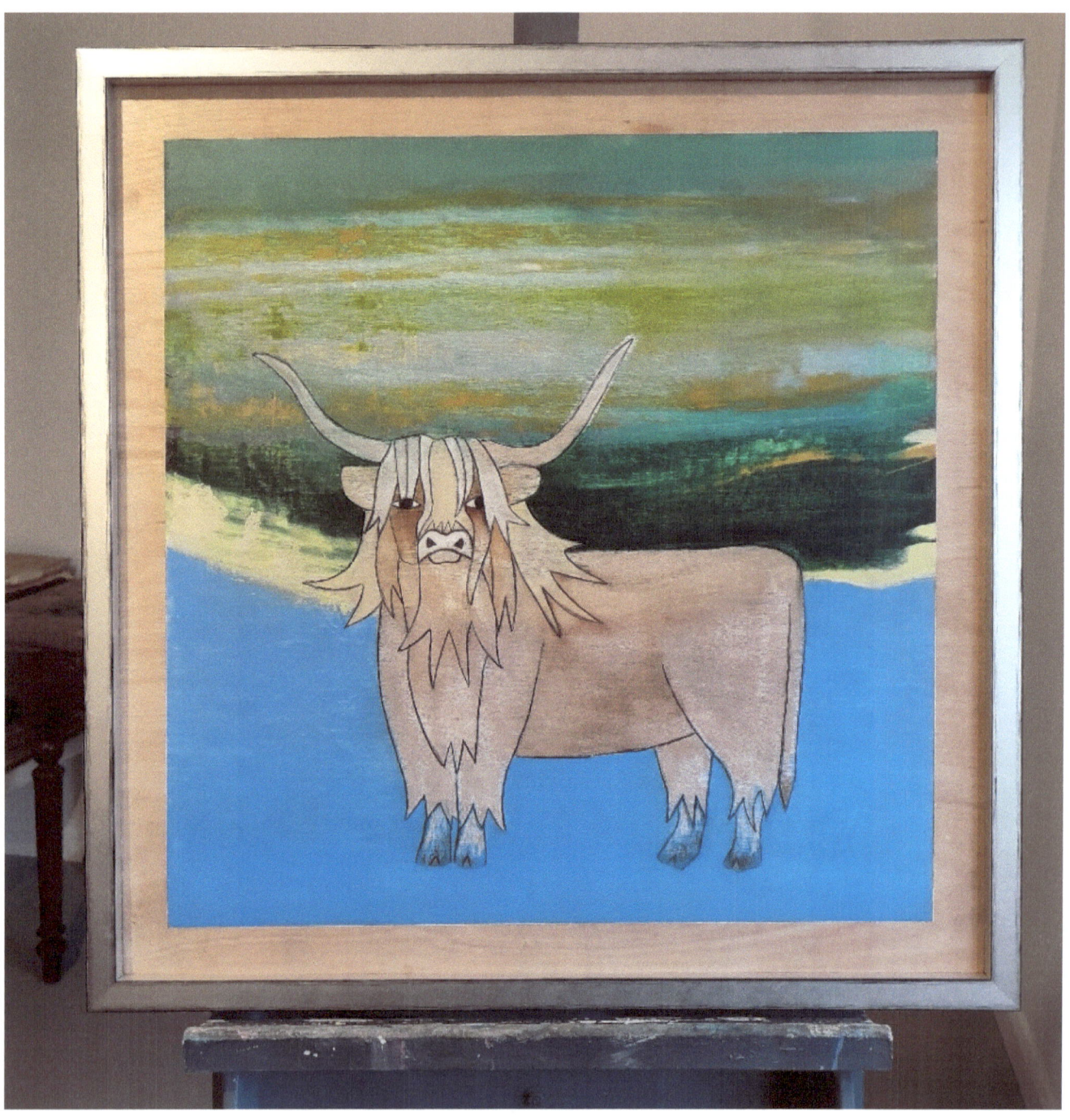

The cow is the symbol of motherhood, mother Gaia and mother earth and reminds us to practice the arts of care, kindness and serenity.

# Ginger Highland Coo

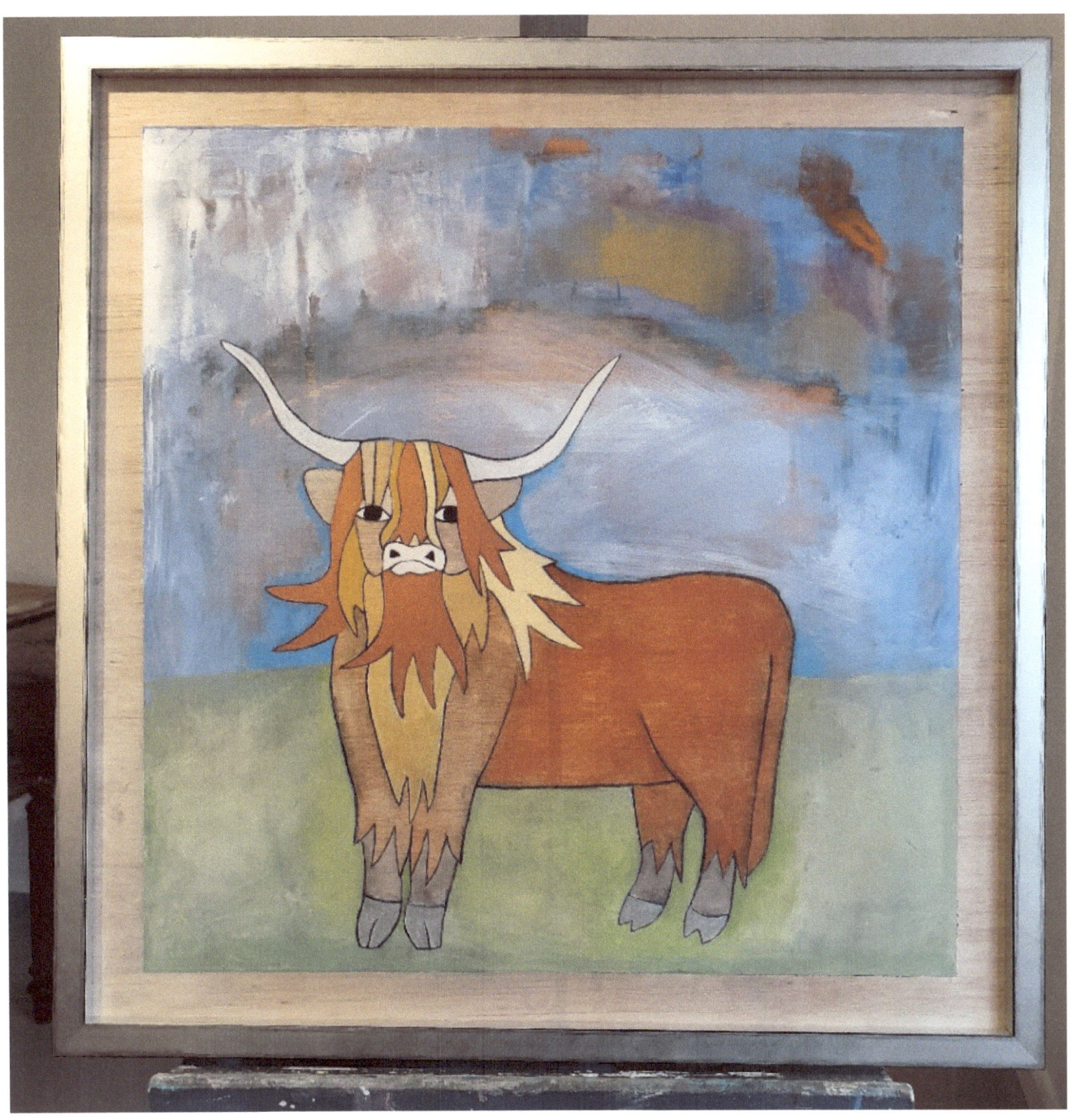

The cow spirit animal is a powerful symbol of nurturing, abundance and gentleness.

# Highland Coo Nighttime

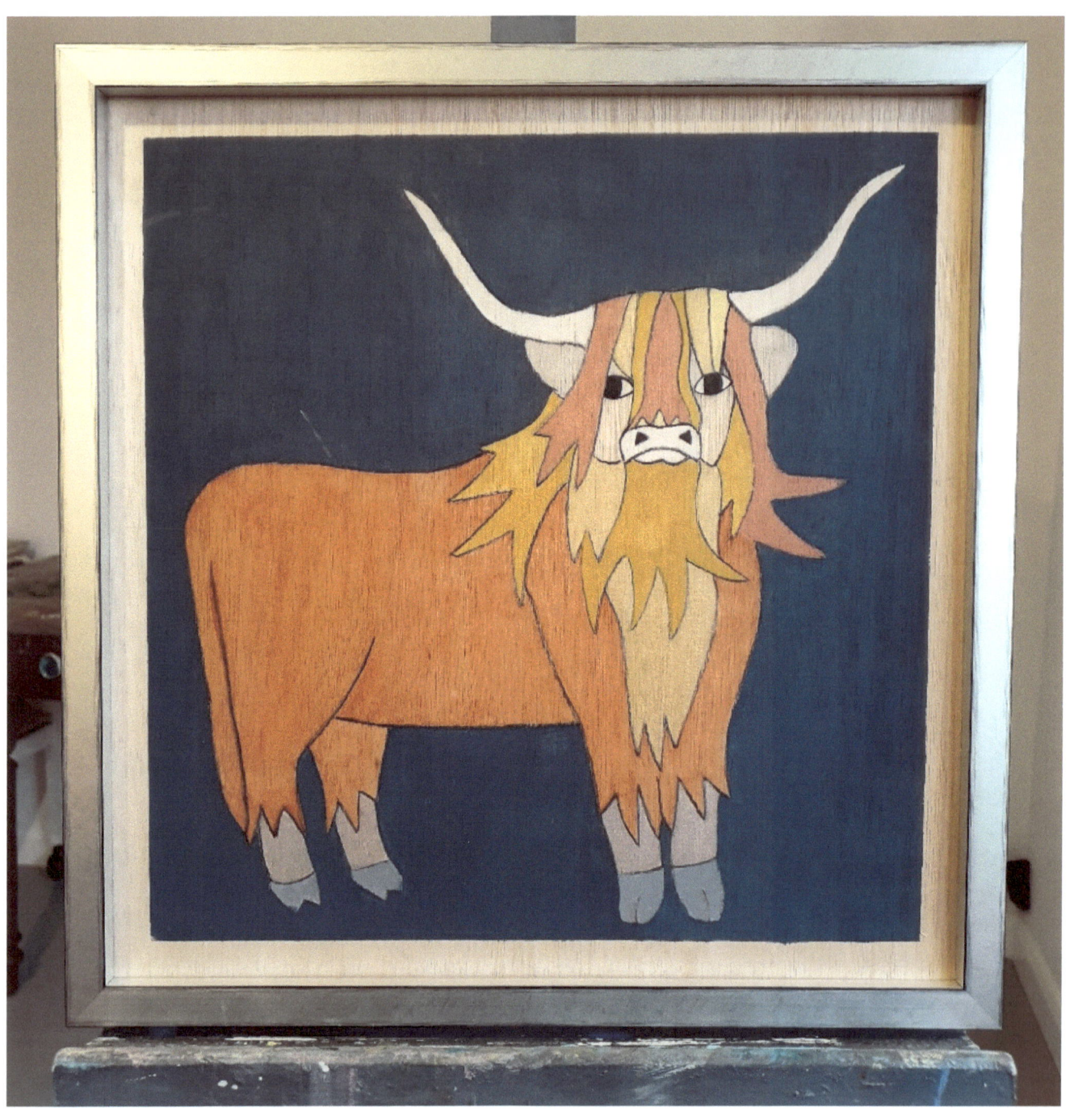

By embracing the qualities and lessons of the cow,
we can cultivate a life of harmony, prosperity, and peace.

# Calm dog

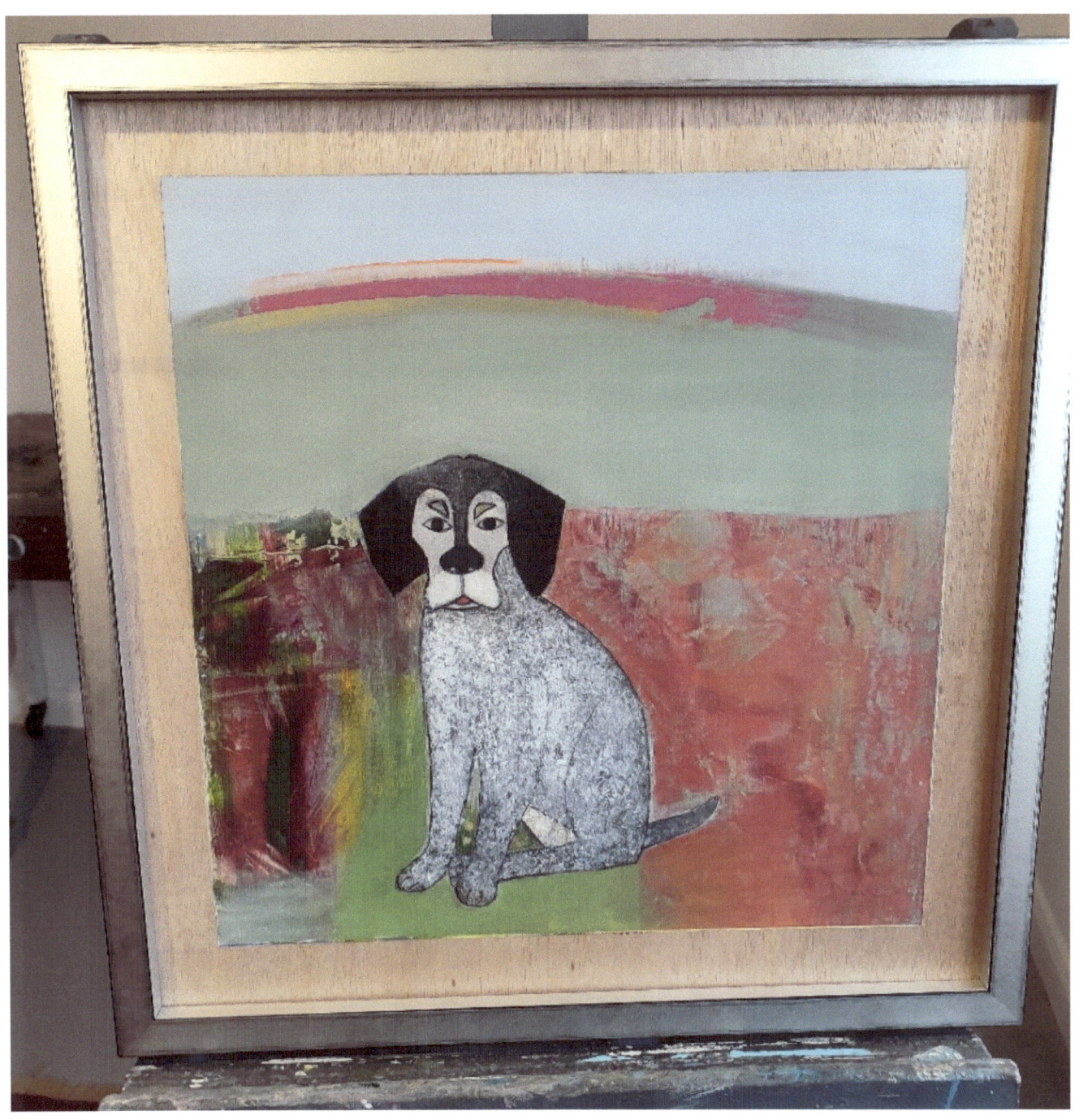

A dog is a heart healer and helps reduce stress and anxiety.

# Tall dog

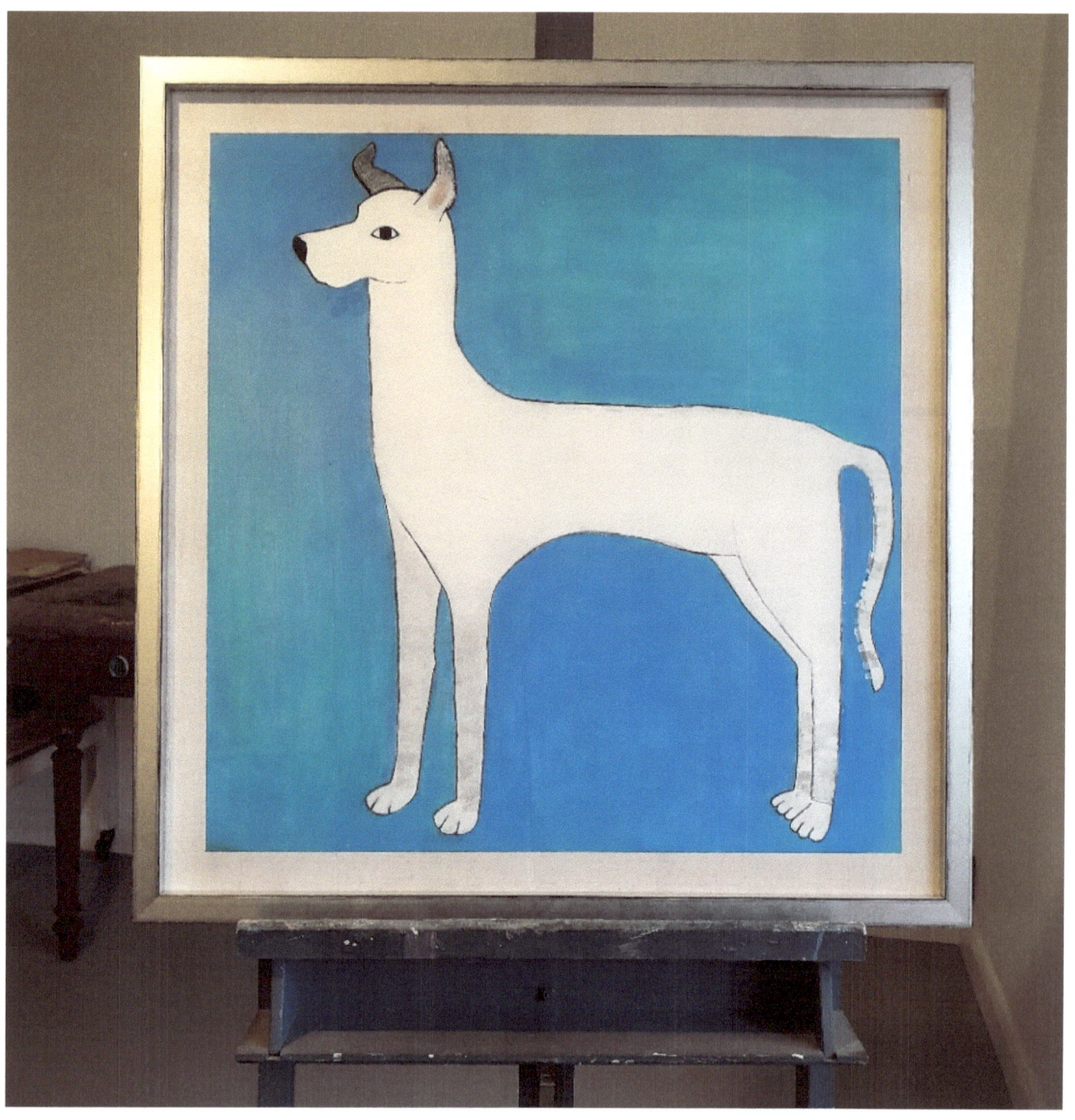

Dogs are well known for their steadfast devotion to their human companions.

# Mans Best Friend

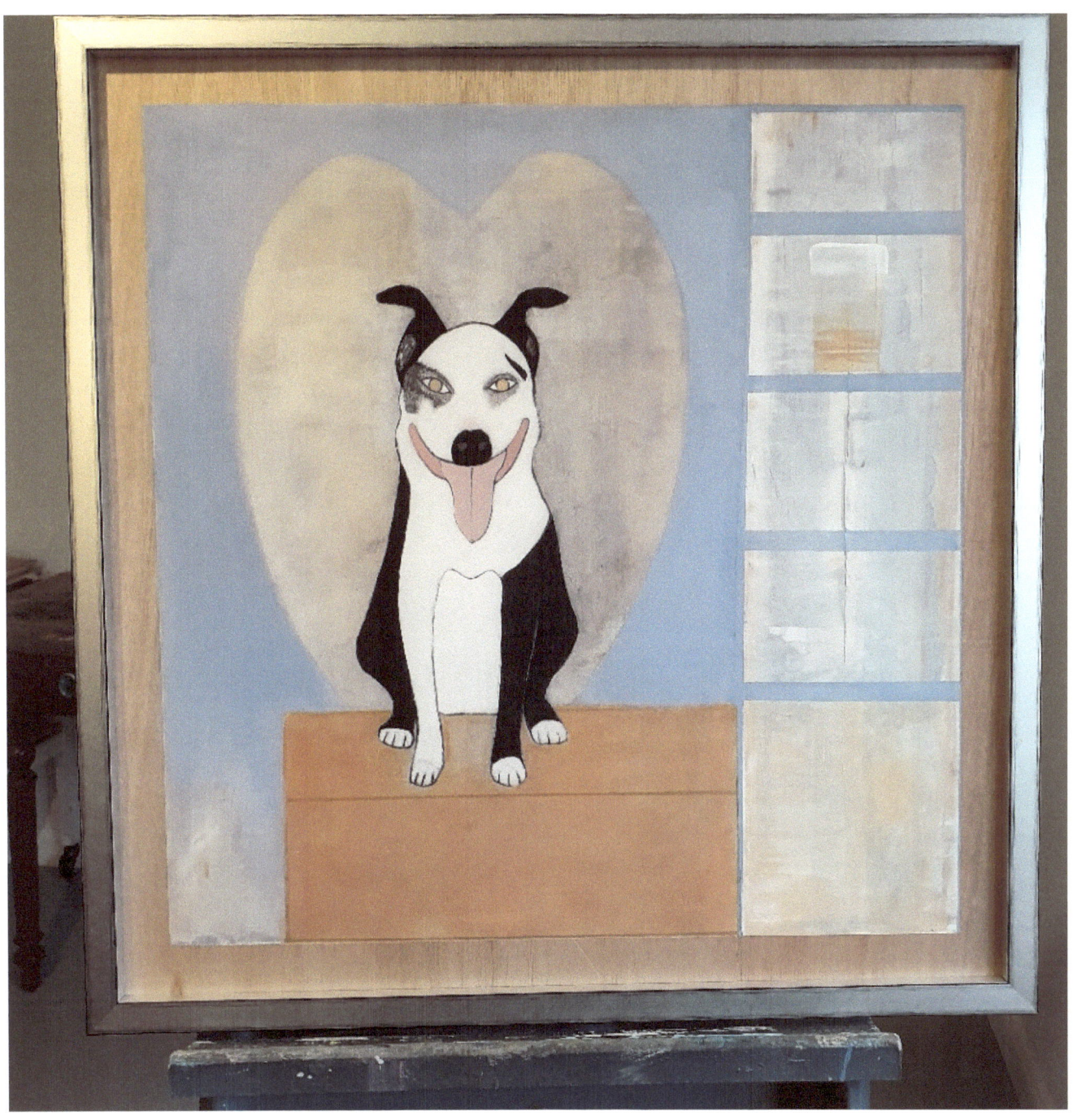

The dog symbolises friendship, love and protection.

# Badger

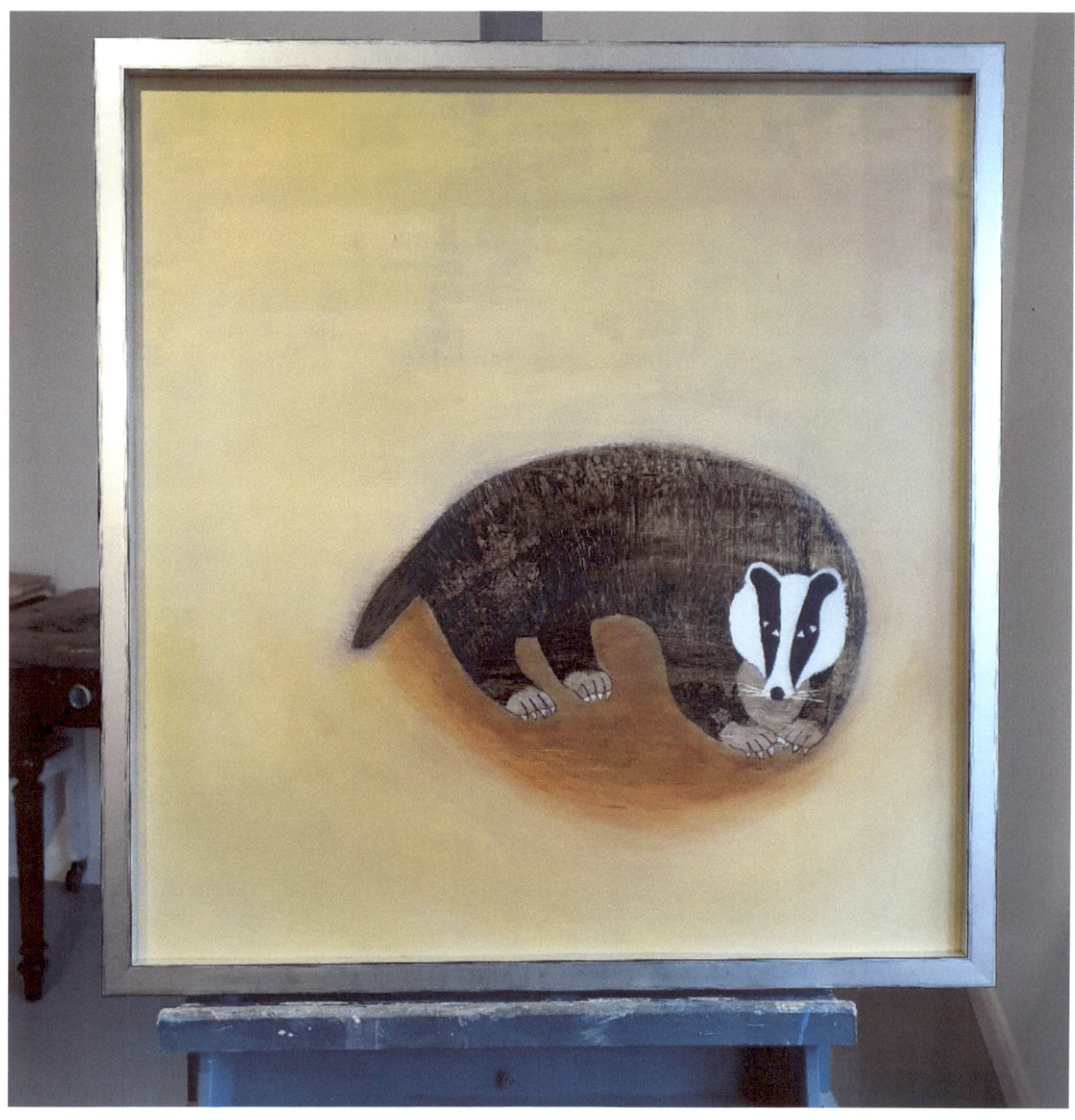

The badger as a healing totem is defensive of self and family. It symbolises strength and self reliance.

# Badger

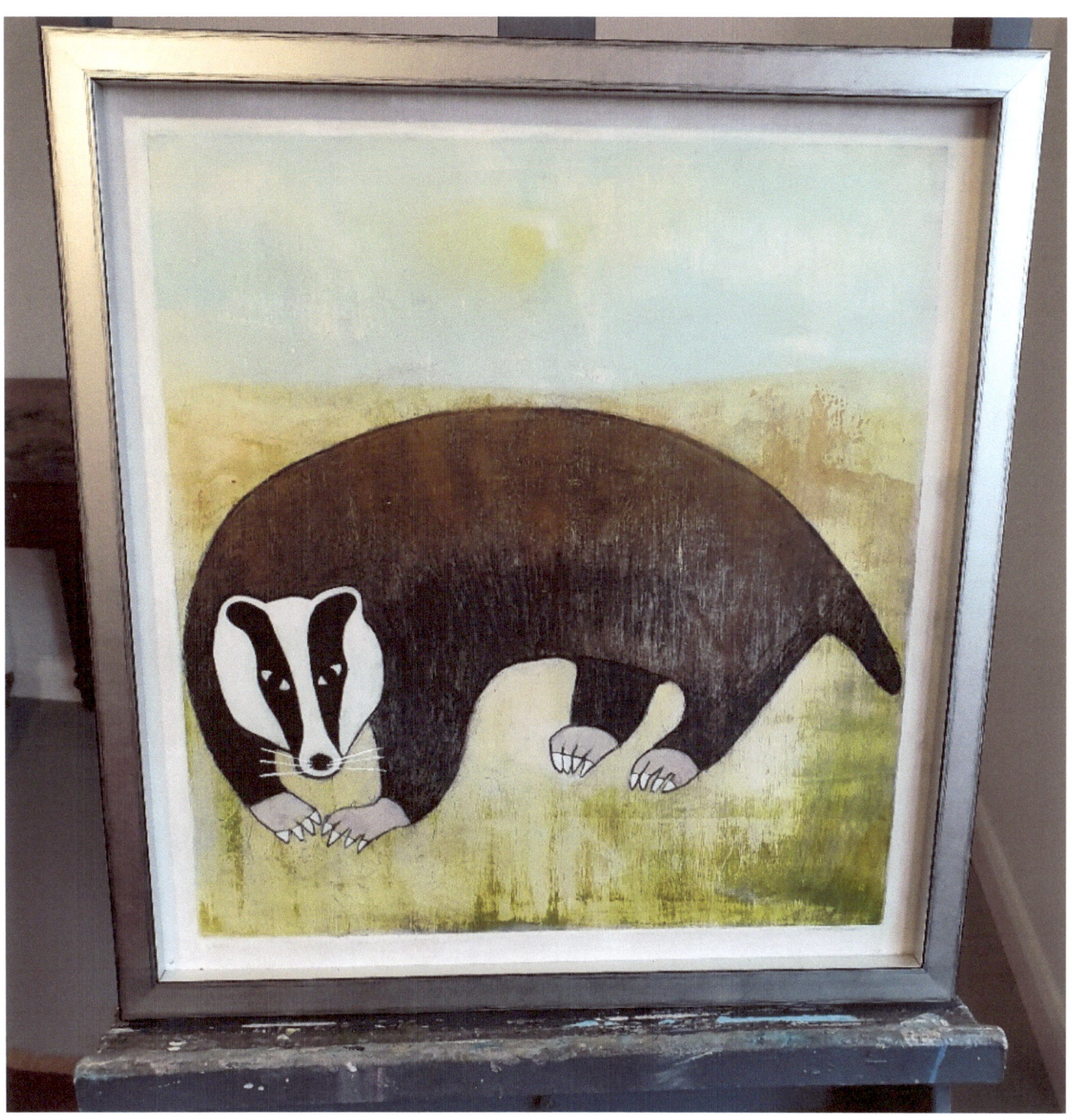

The badger totem brings with it magical wisdom and interest.

# Bees on Flower

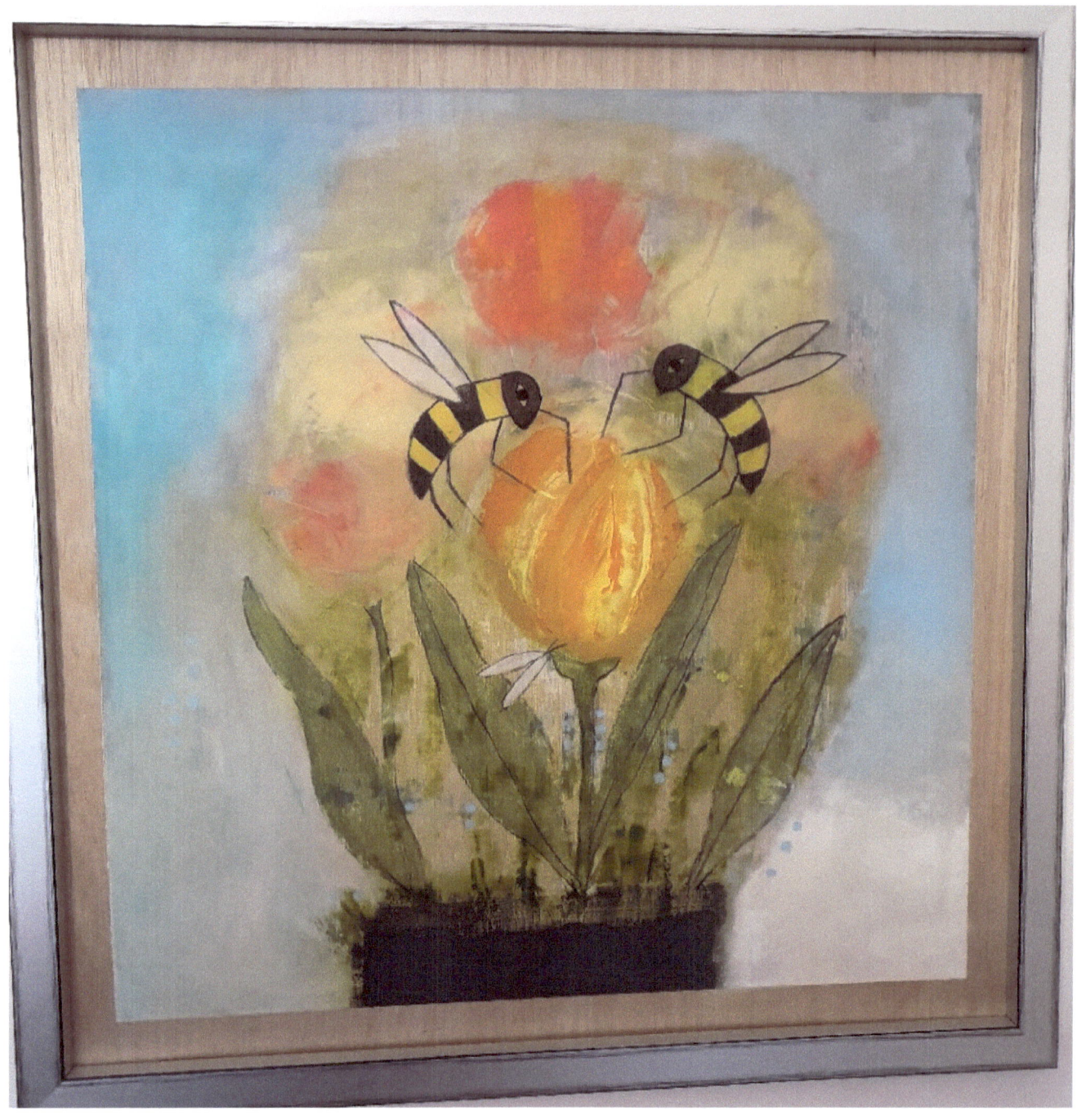

Honey bees serve an integral and deeply sacred role in the earths balance.

# Bees

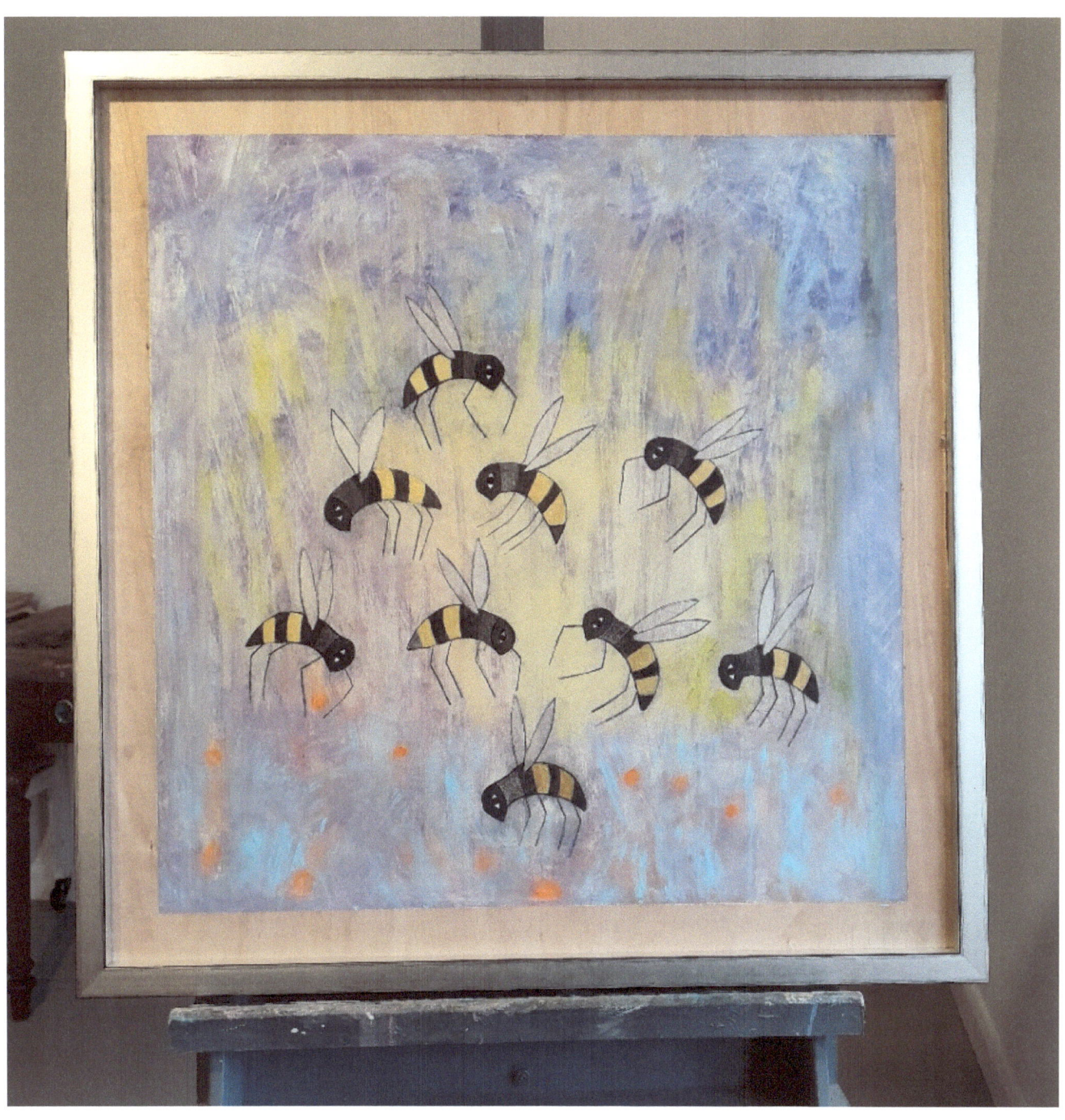

As a spirit totem they inspire unity, diligence and resilience.

# Rooster on Blue

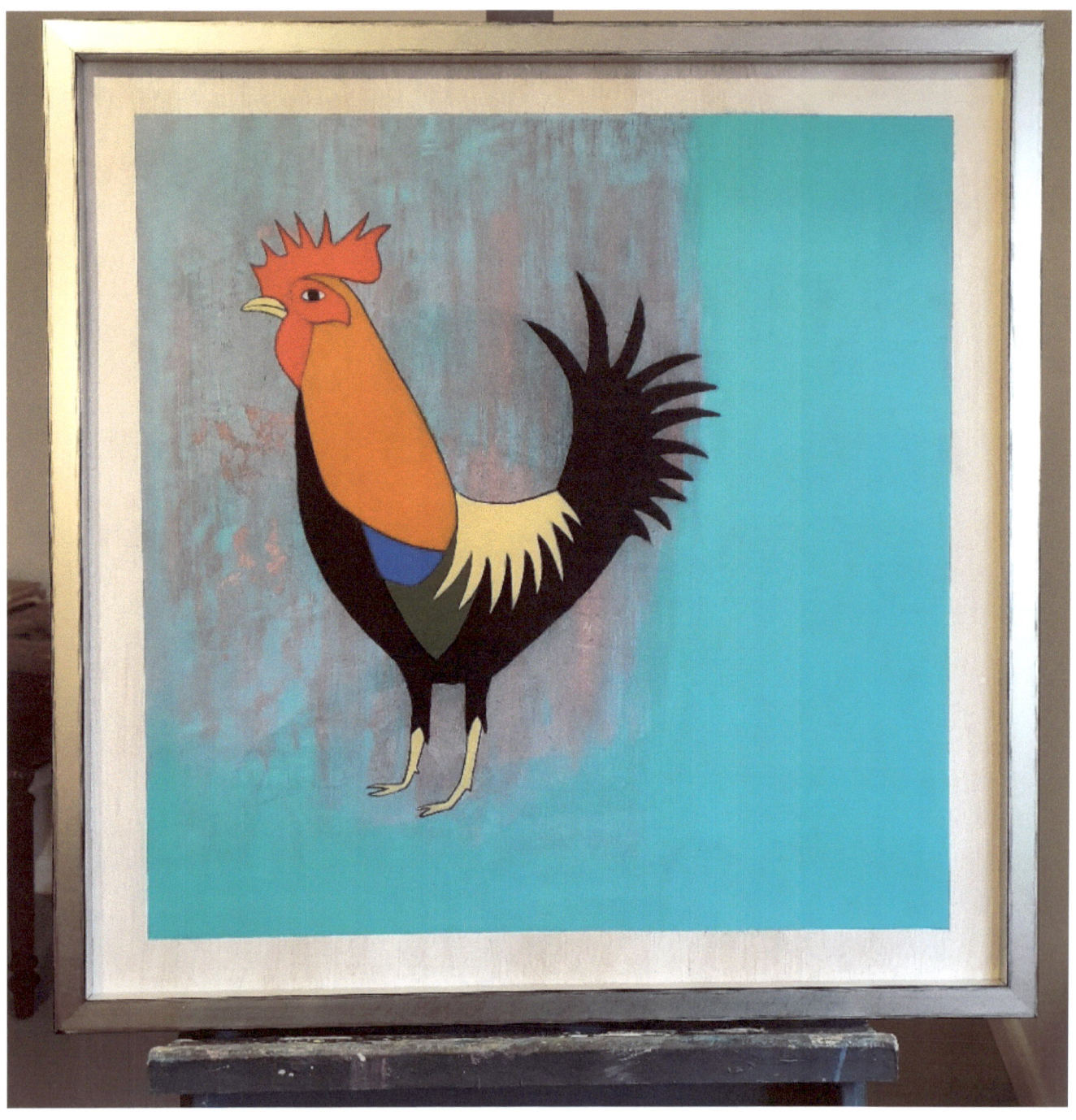

Rooster gives you hope and mental keenness ..

Rooster is a totem animal, helps you to be a potent protector who is adept at keeping negative energies and evil away with your solar light which burns brightly in your aura.

# White Rooster

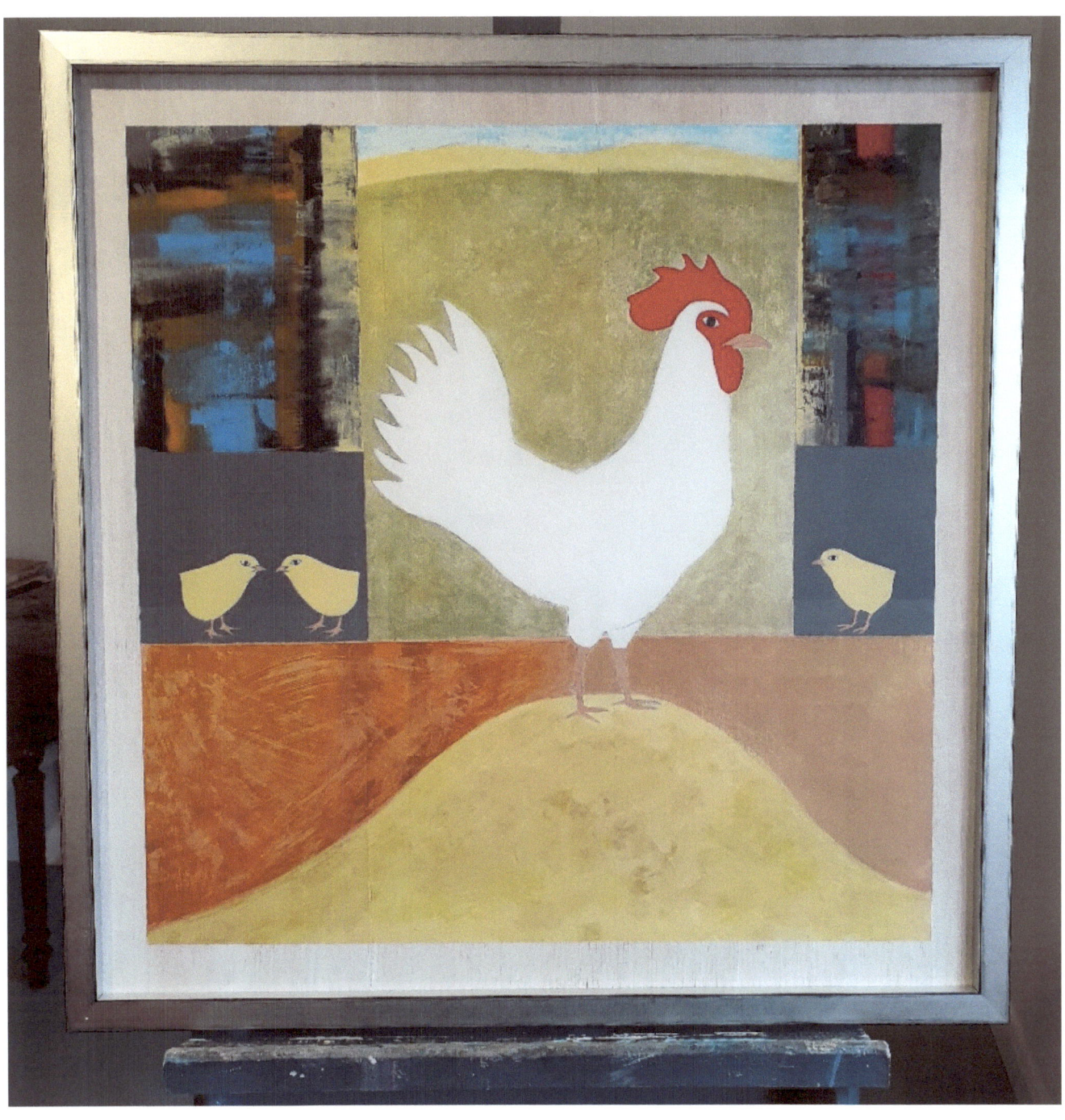

As rooster arches his neck up to the heavens and lets loose his sacred song, our attention is drawn to the fact that we are alive

# Rooster and Chicks

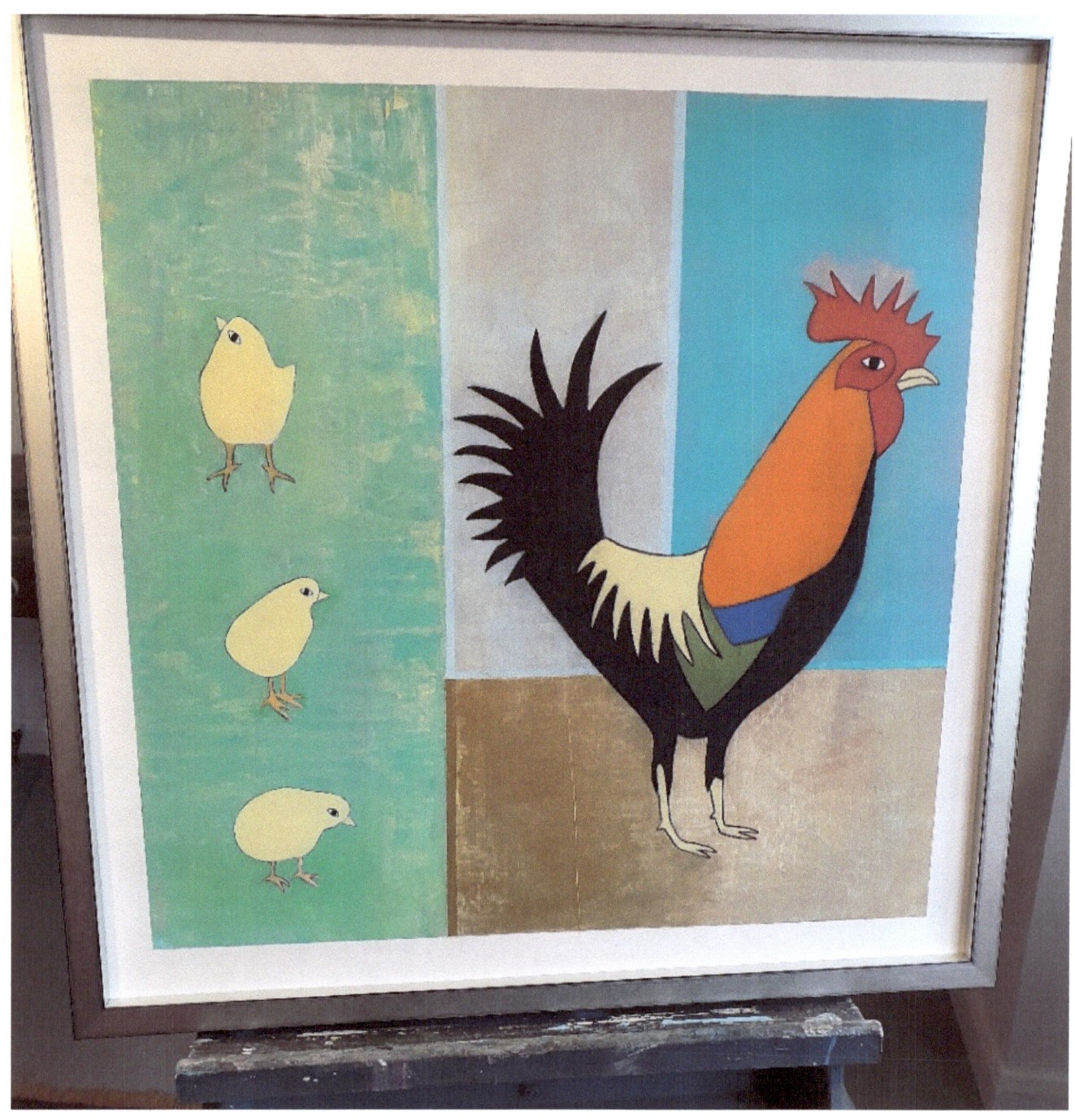

The rooster believes that he is entitled to touch the stars.

# Cat

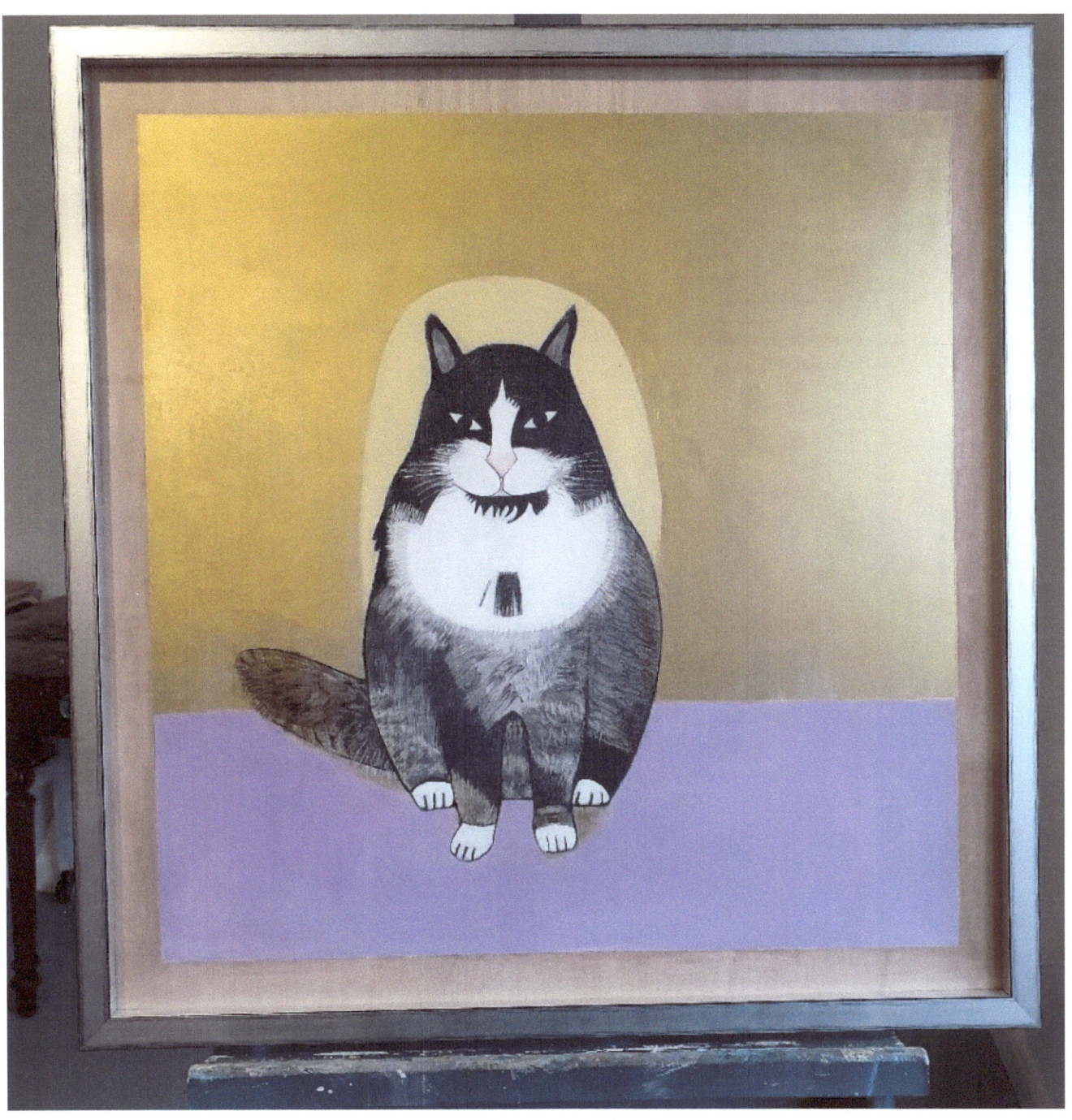

The cat symbolises individuality and stubbornness, and offers protection from dark forces as they walk between the physical and spiritual world.

# Swimmer

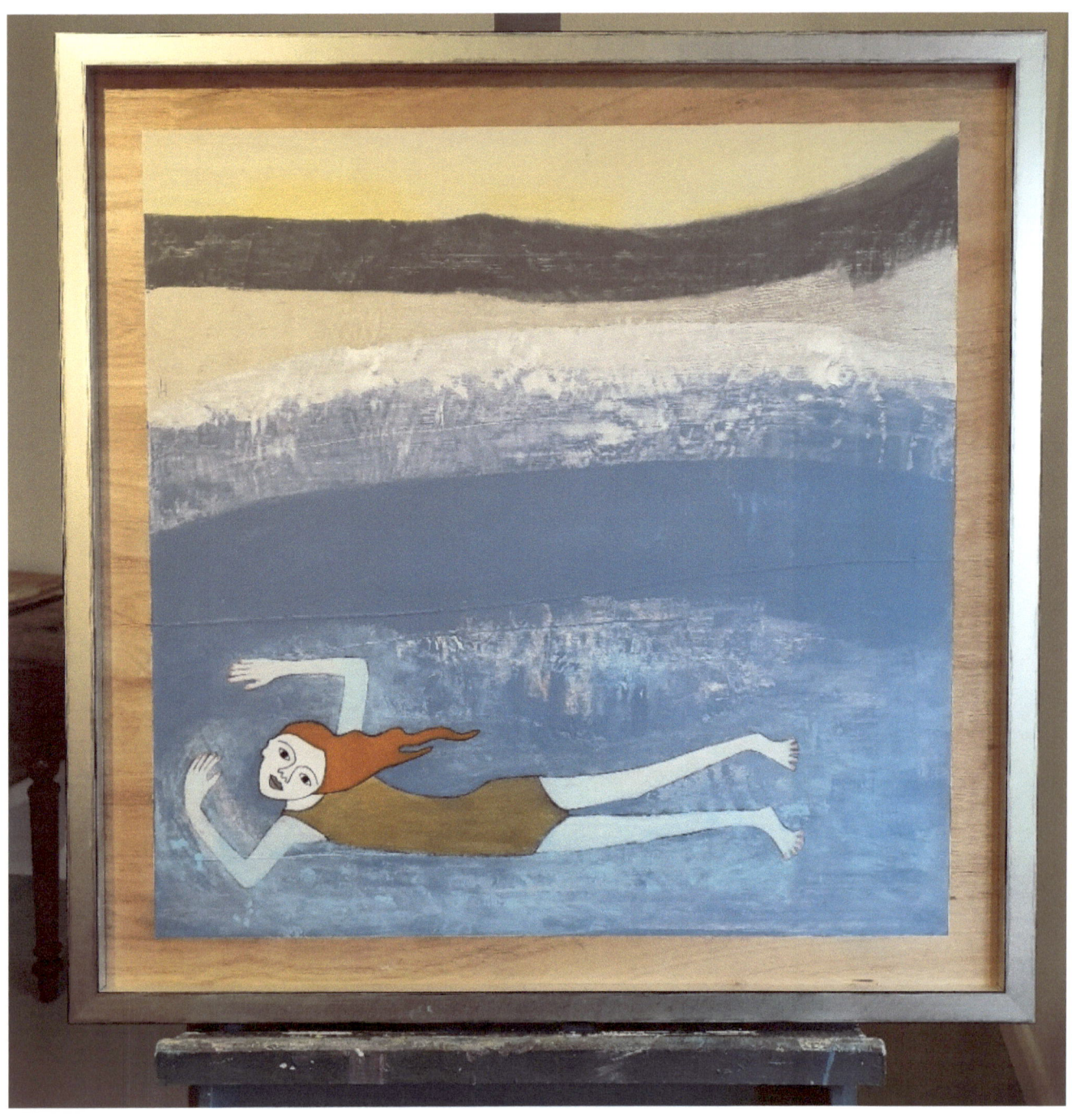

Swimming changes lives, the thrill of plunging or dipping  a toe in open water brings joy, confidence, adventure and friendship. It can wash away stress  and sadness, pain and grief.

Water is a healer, a place to feel gloriously and elementally alive and in touch with yourself, with others, and with nature.

# Seagulls

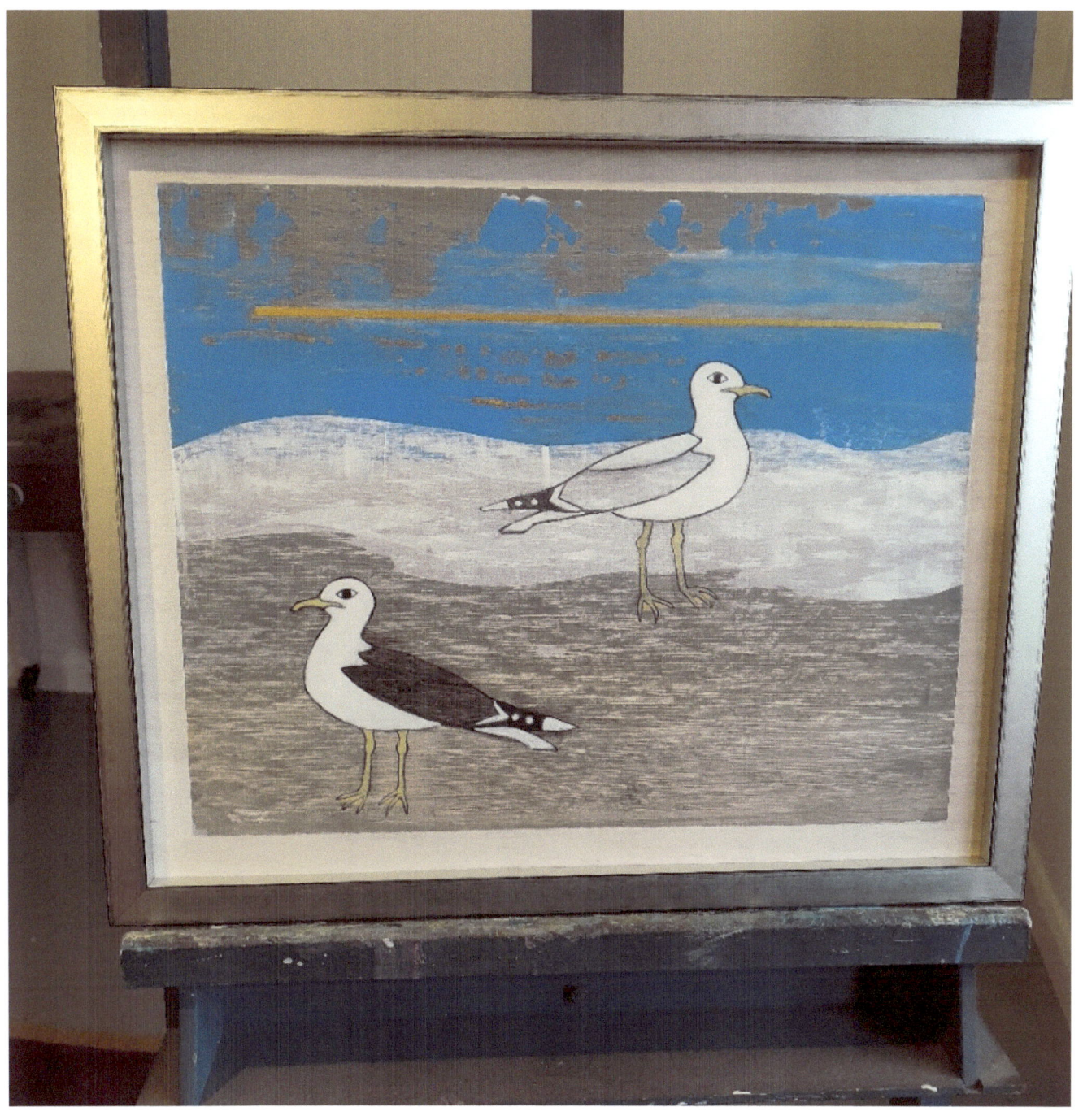

The seagulls inspire one to persevere and survive through crises, let go of worry, go with the flow, and enjoy oneself.

# Seagull over Beach

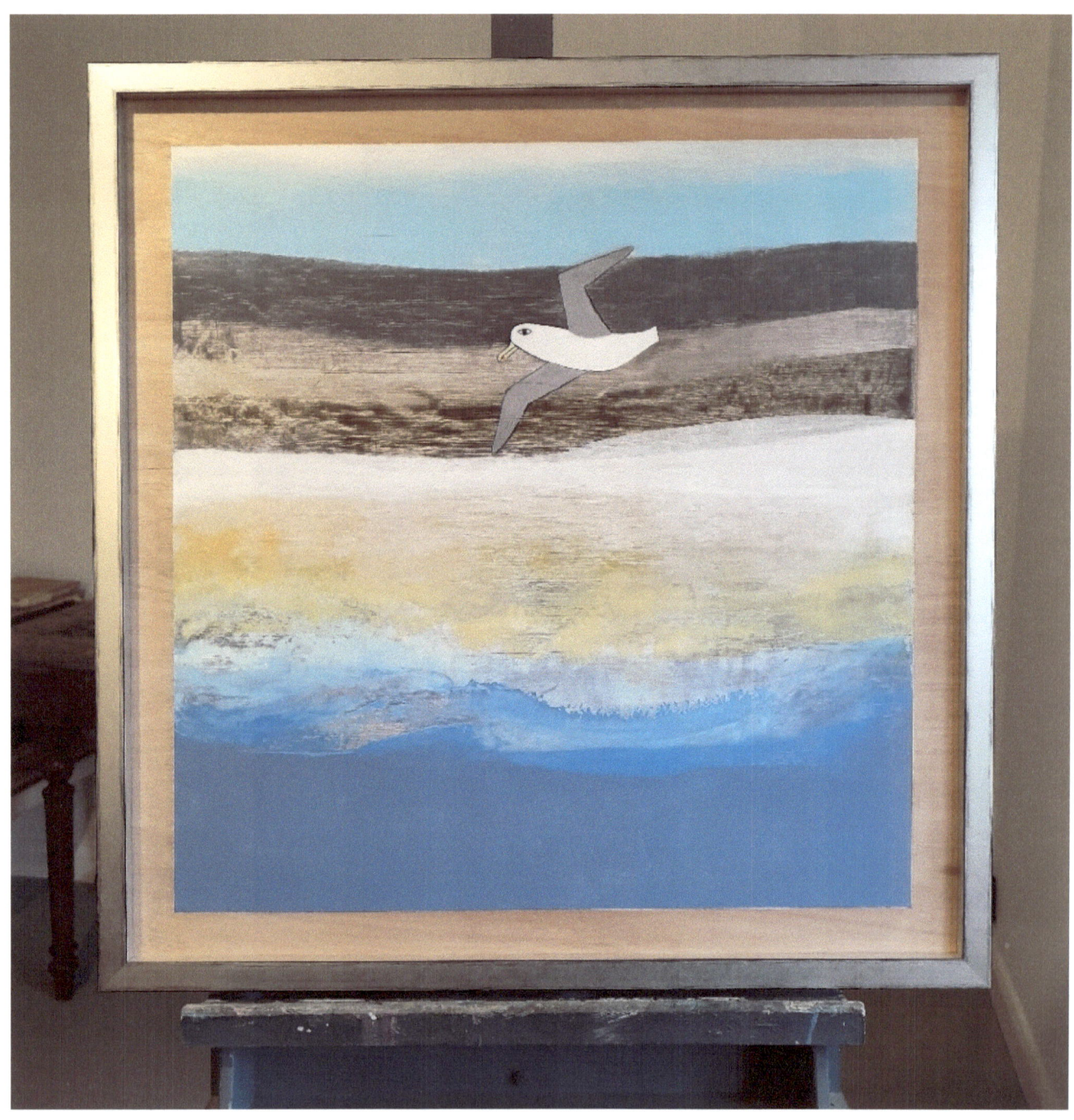

The seagull as a spirit animal represents a free spirited nature and a love of adventures and exploring new horizons.

# Dove

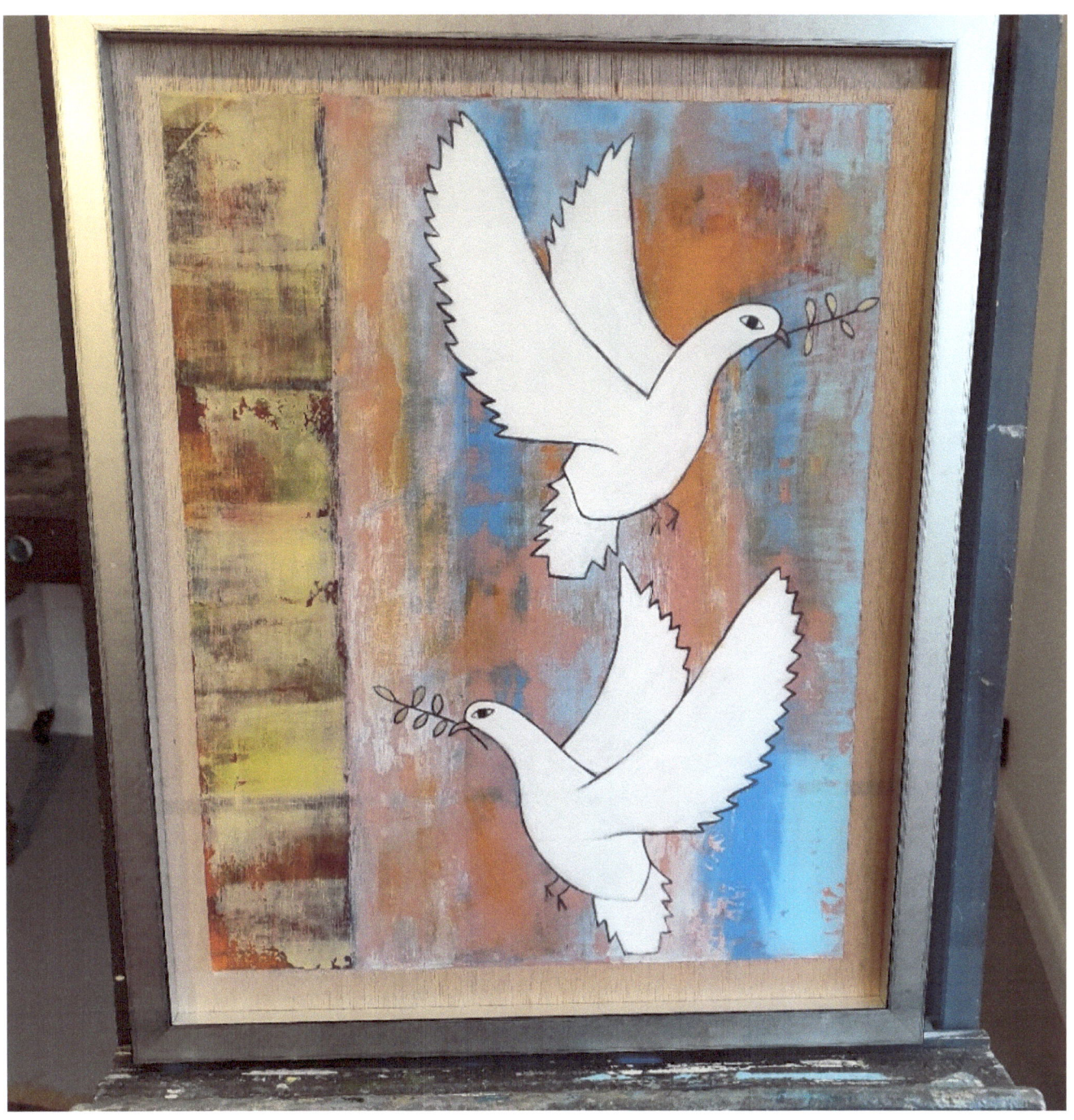

The dove is a symbol of hope, purity, faith and peace.

# Dove on wood

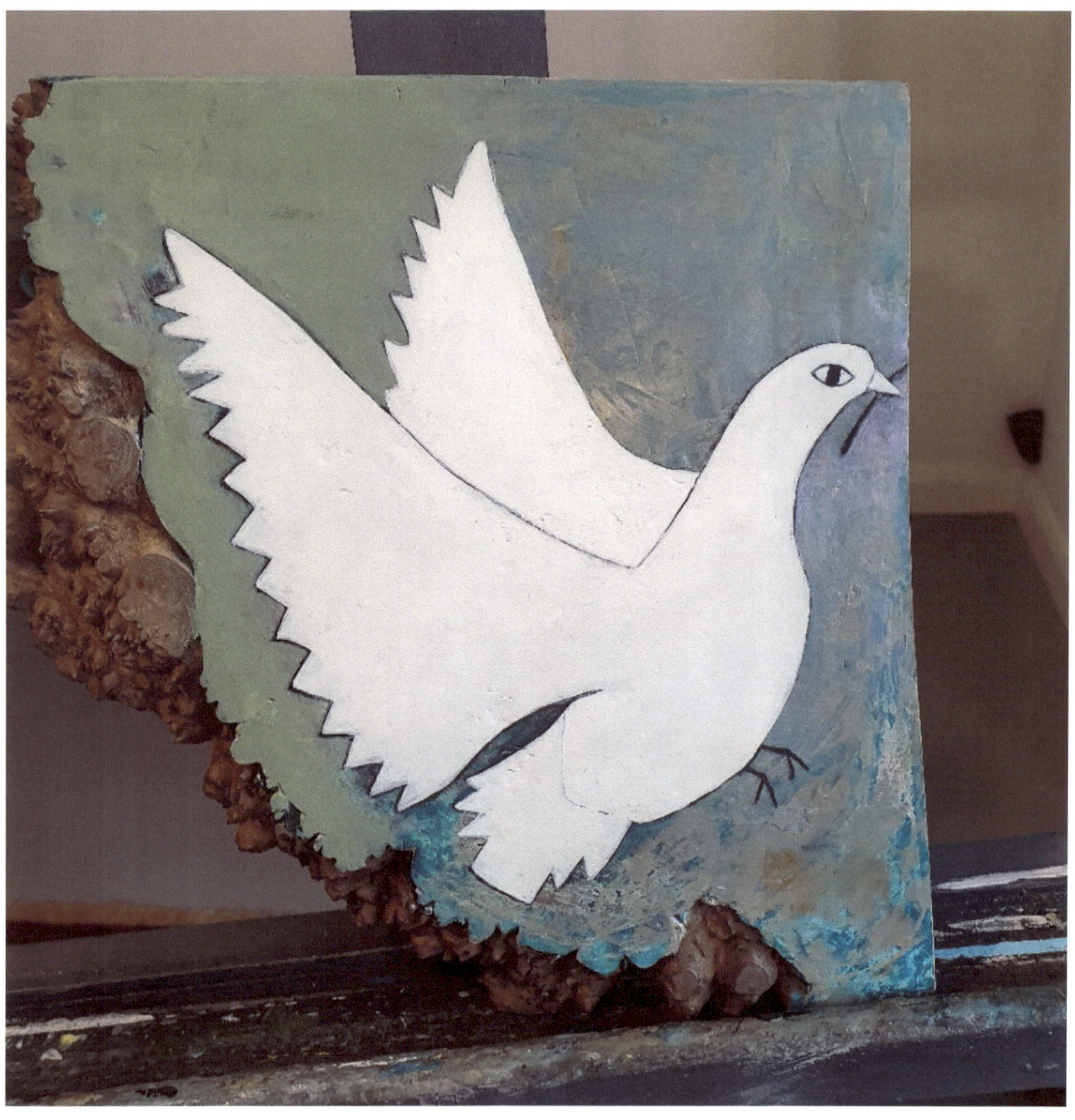

Doves bring healing messages from parted loved ones to our ears.

# Relaxing on the Beach

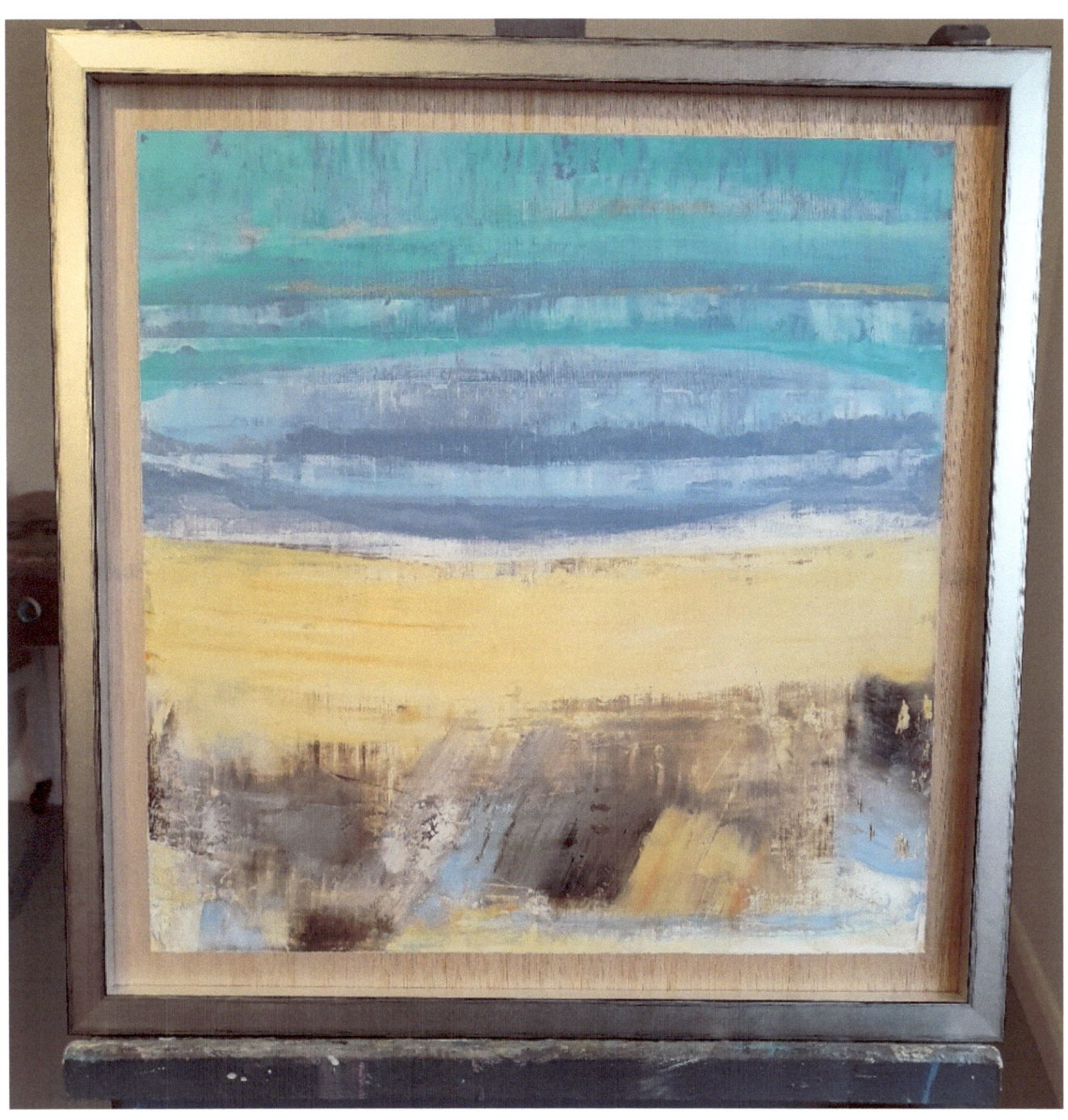

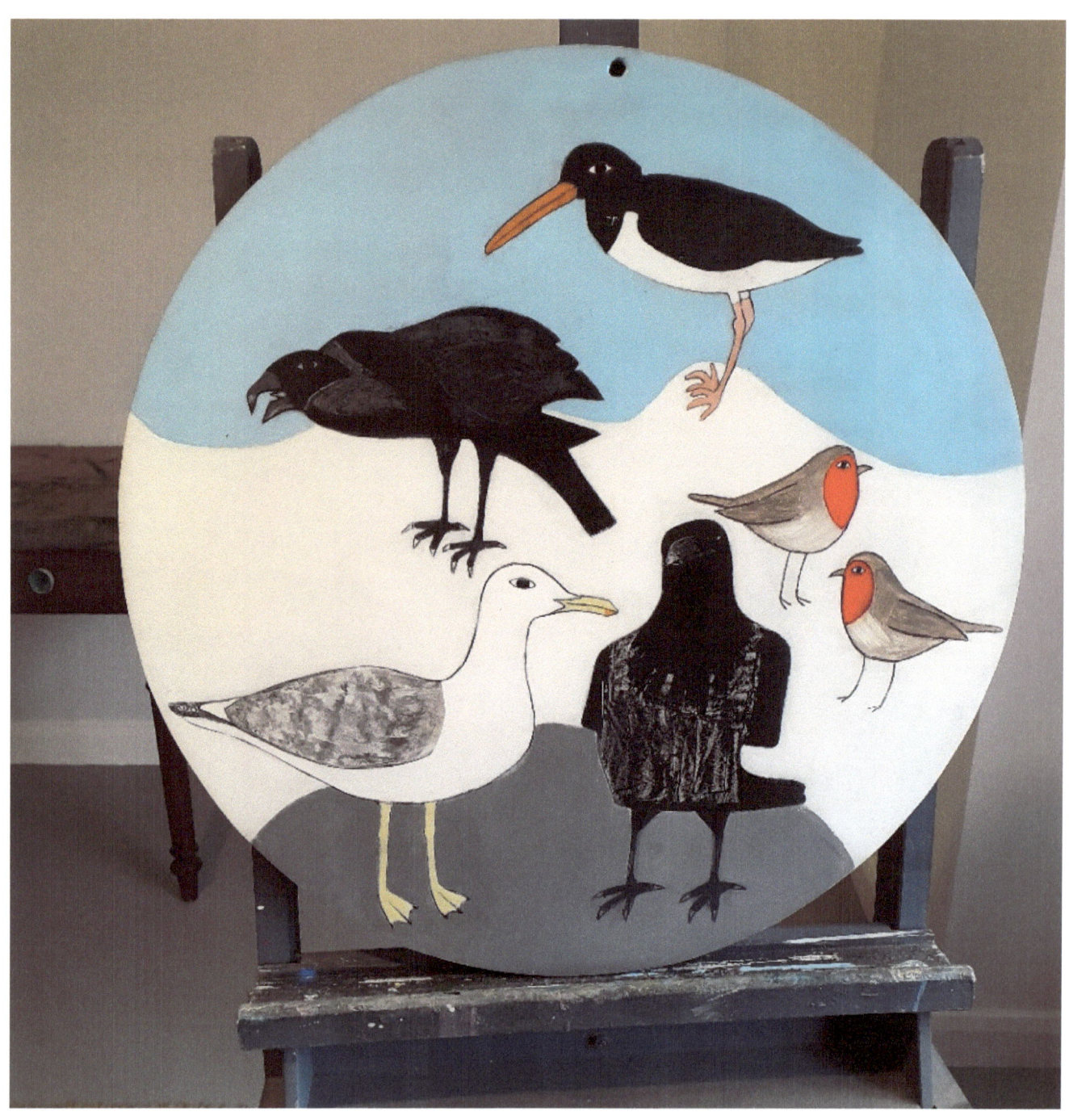

We love to watch the birds.

# Red Squirrel

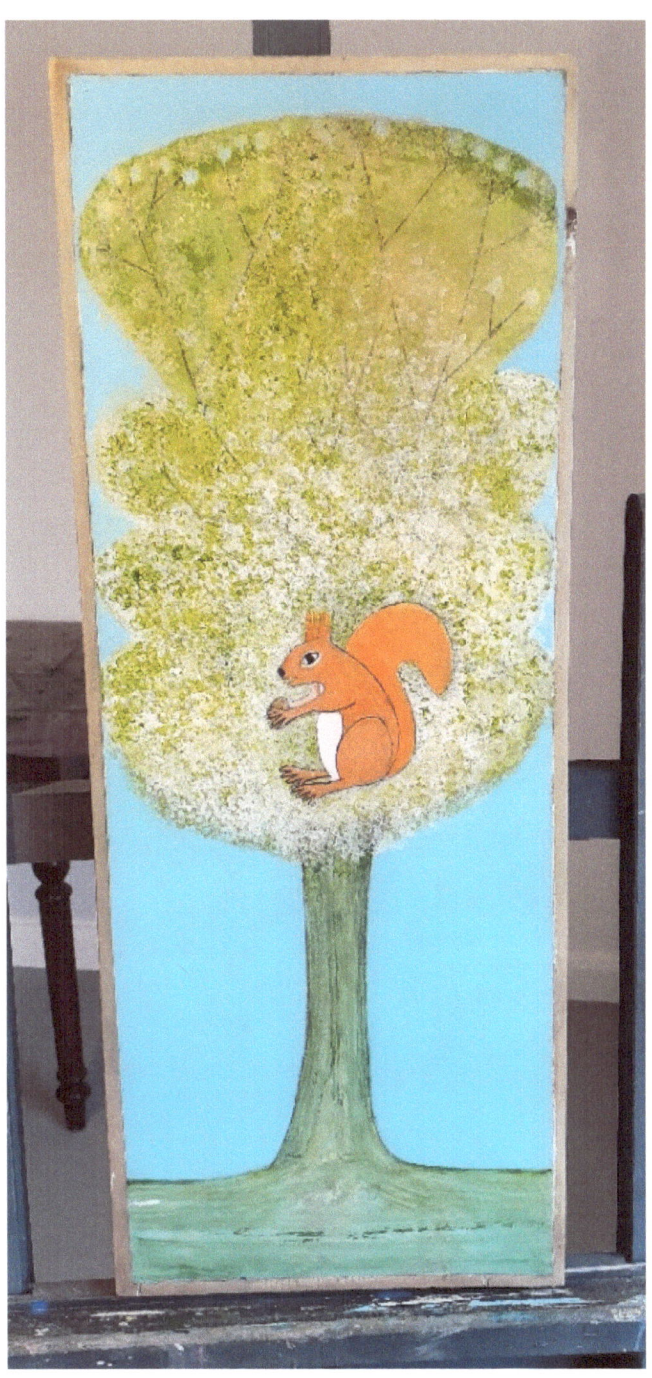

Squirrels are intelligent, resourceful and quick thinkers.

# Snake on Wood

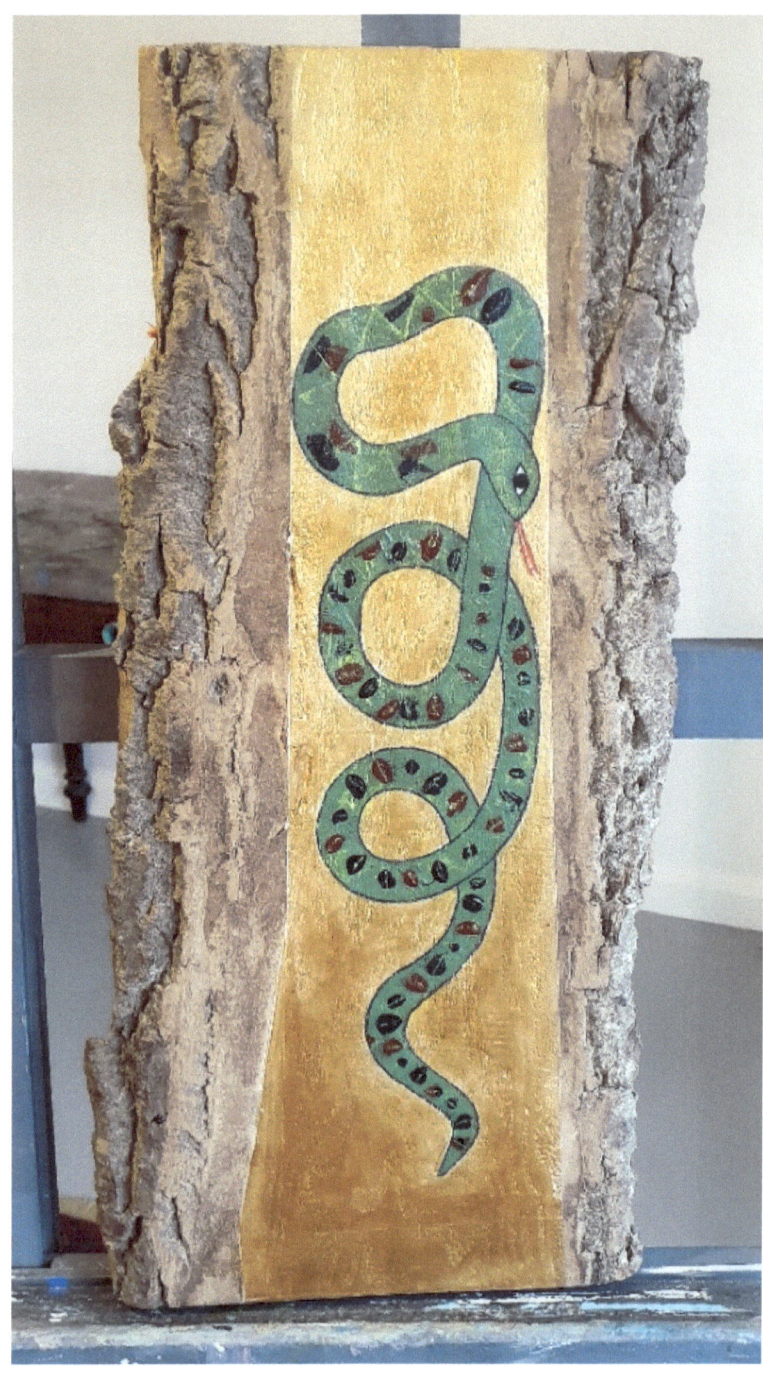

Snake wisdom harnesses its powerful energy to heal and transform.

# Silver Dragon

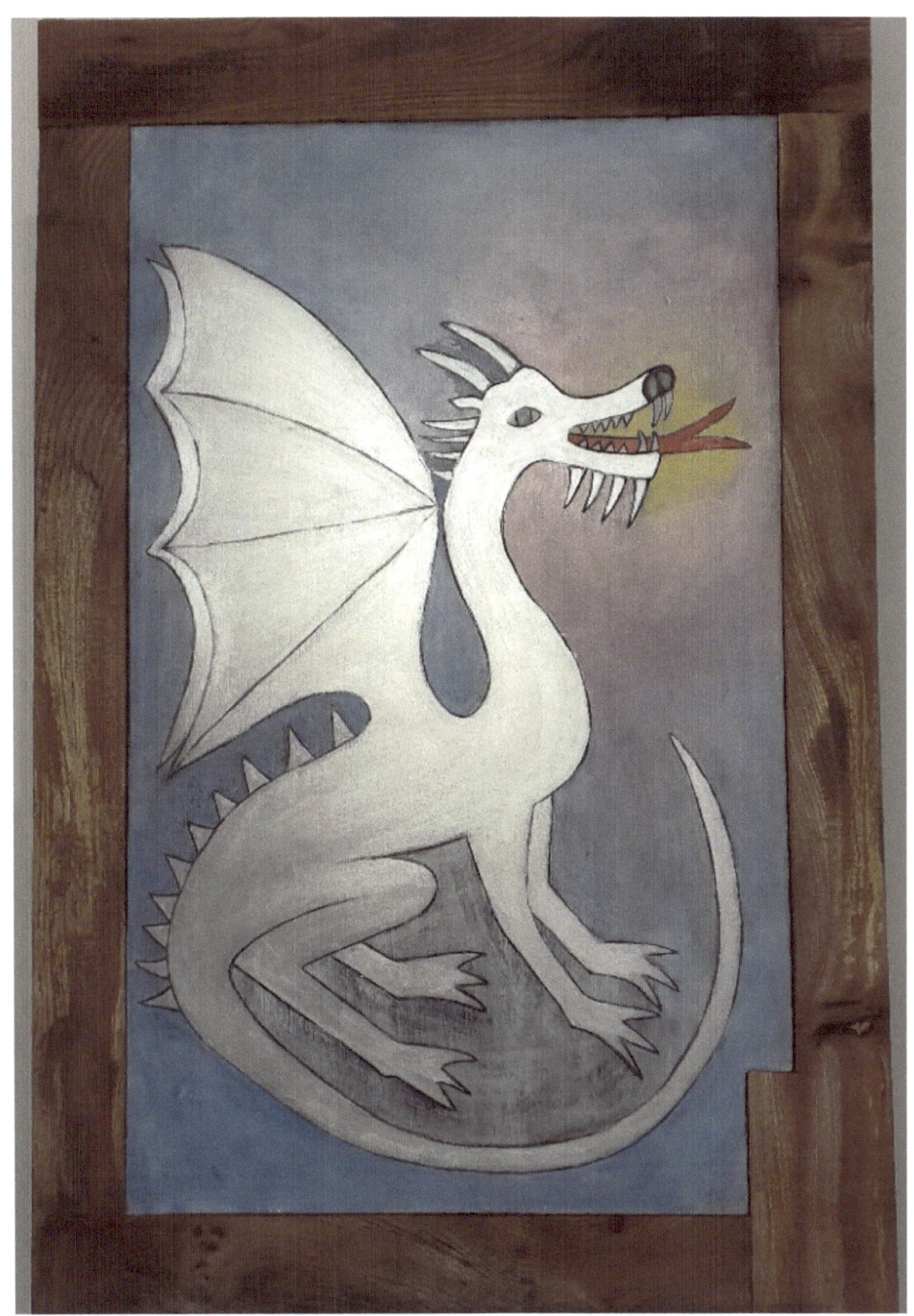

The silver dragon symbolises the divine feminine,
they are wise, calming and gentle.

# Abstract wood

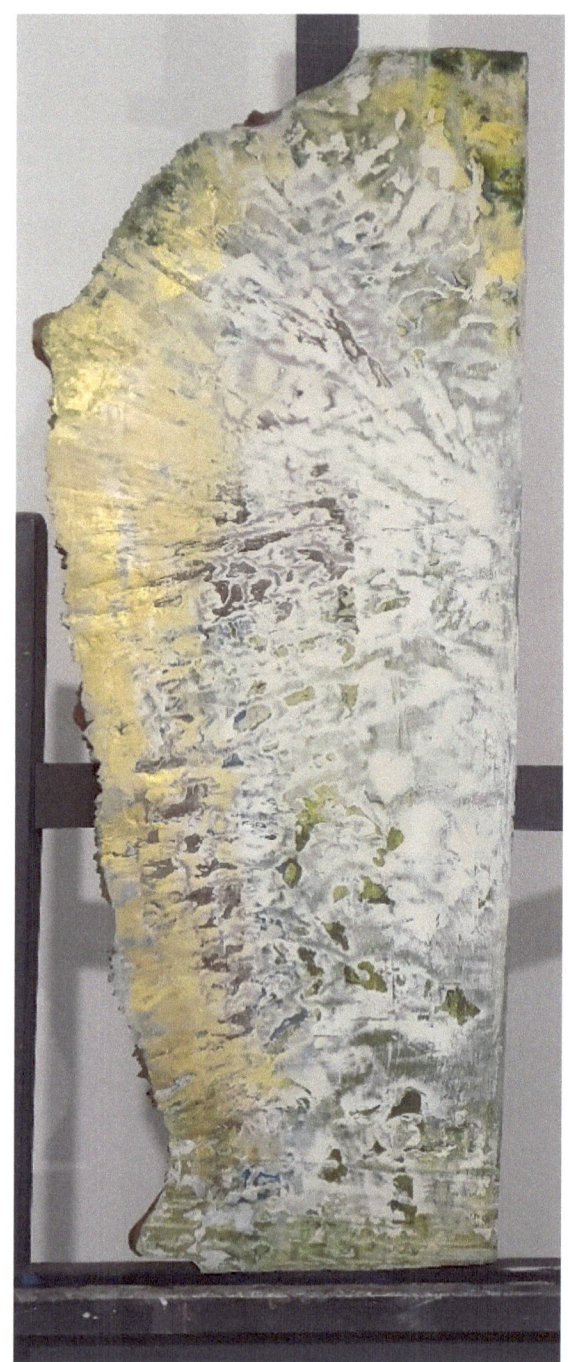

This panel shimmers.

# Candle Flame

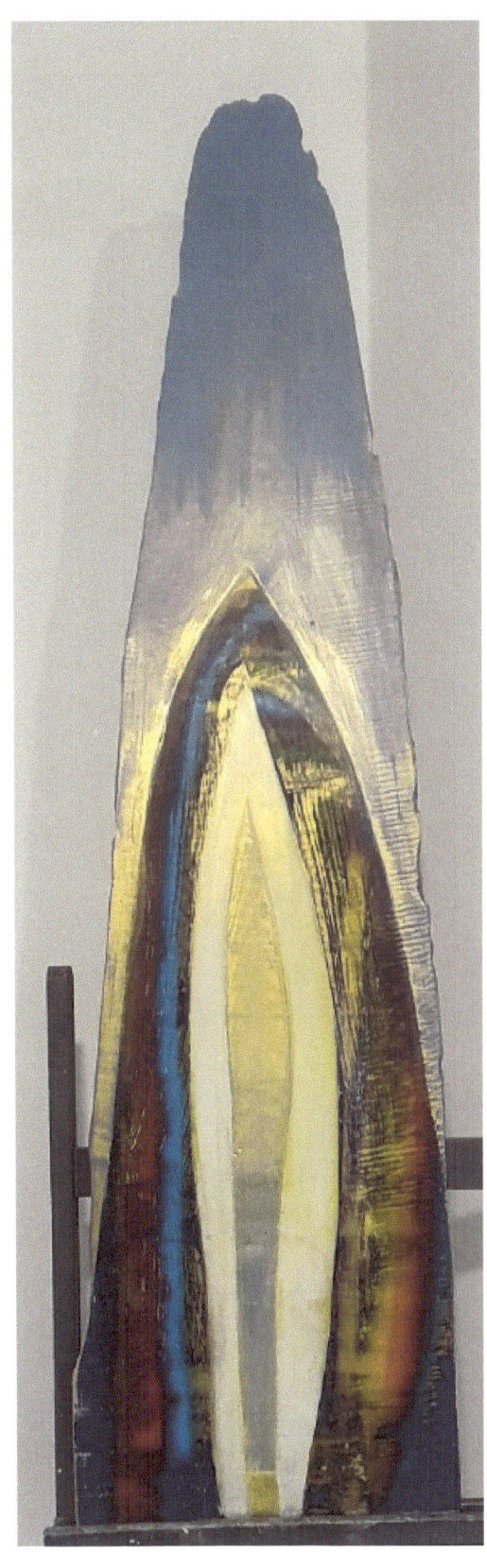

# Seal

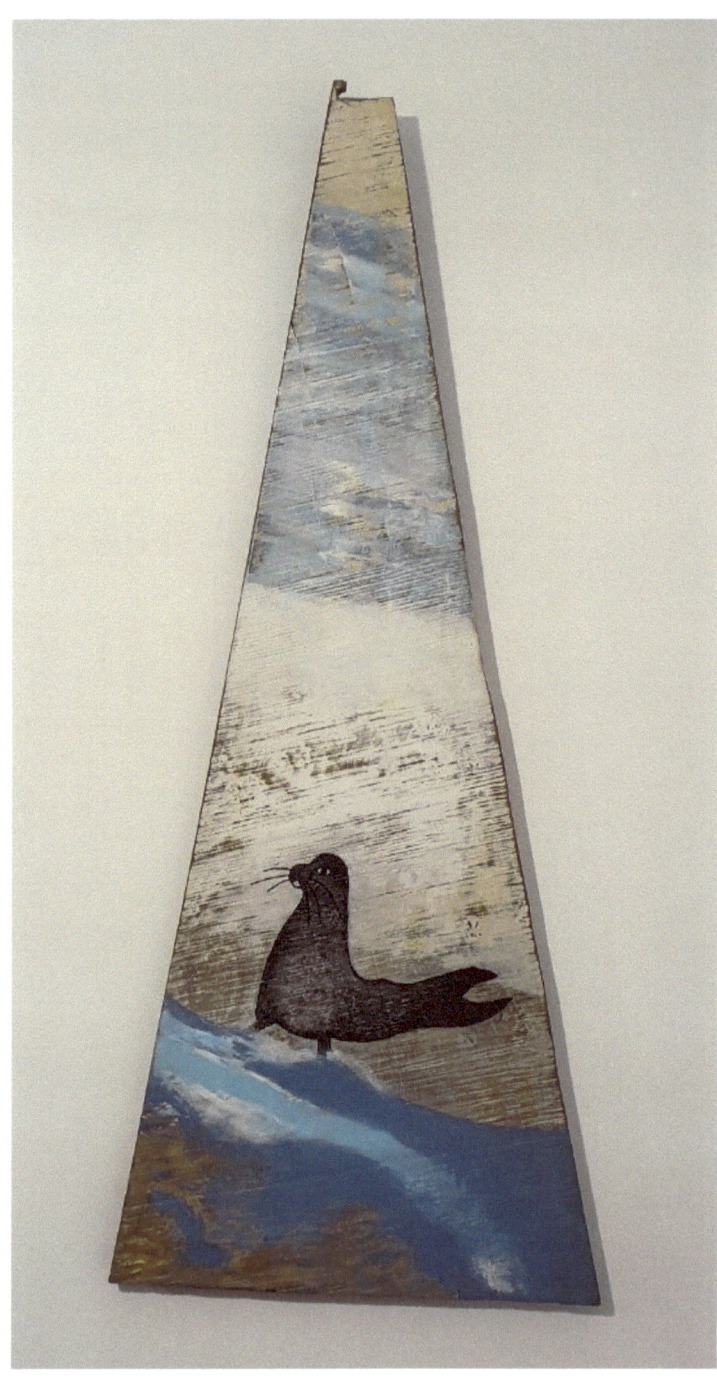

The seal inspires creativity and achieving ones highest potential.

# Mermaid

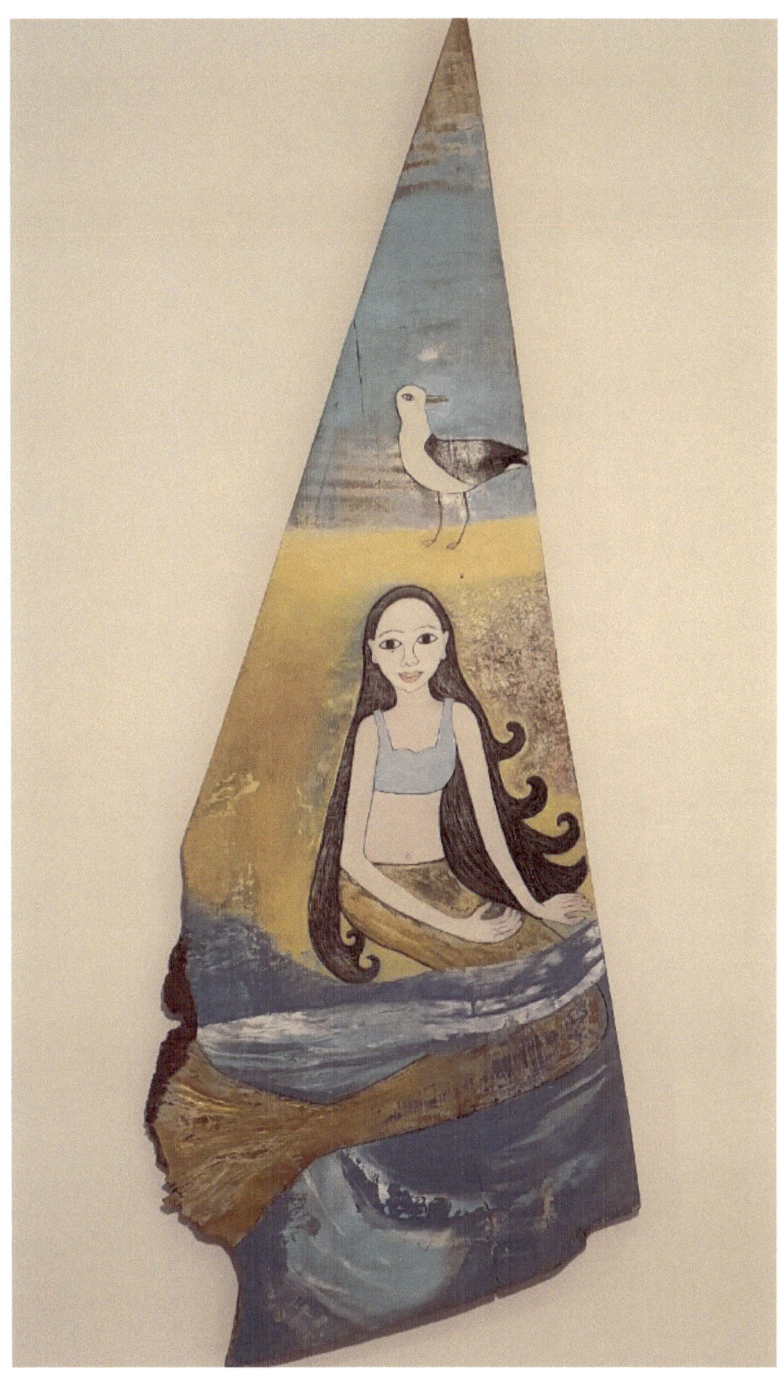

The mermaid inspires one to replace negative emotions with positive ones.

# Buddha

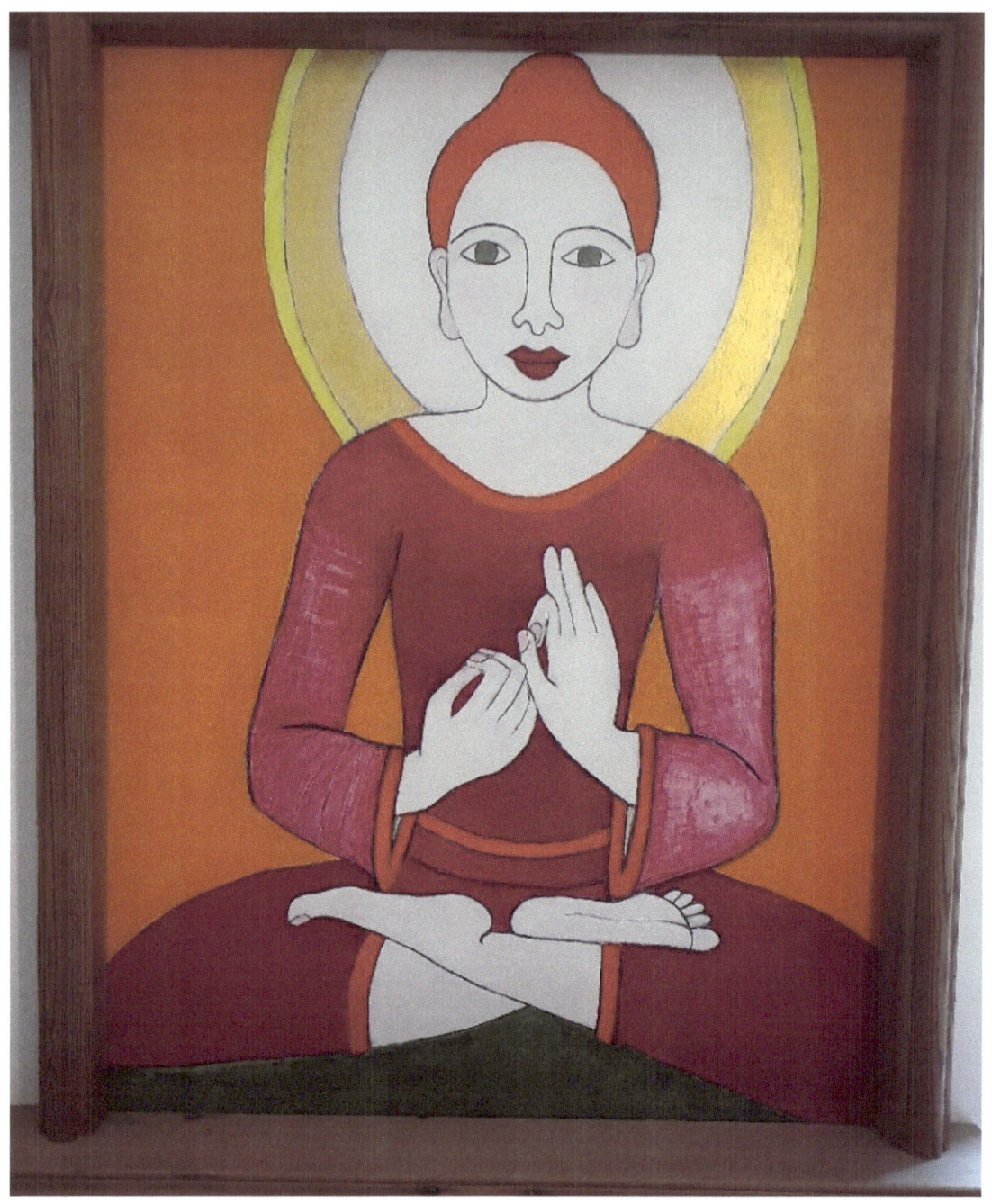

# Dog with Ice Cream

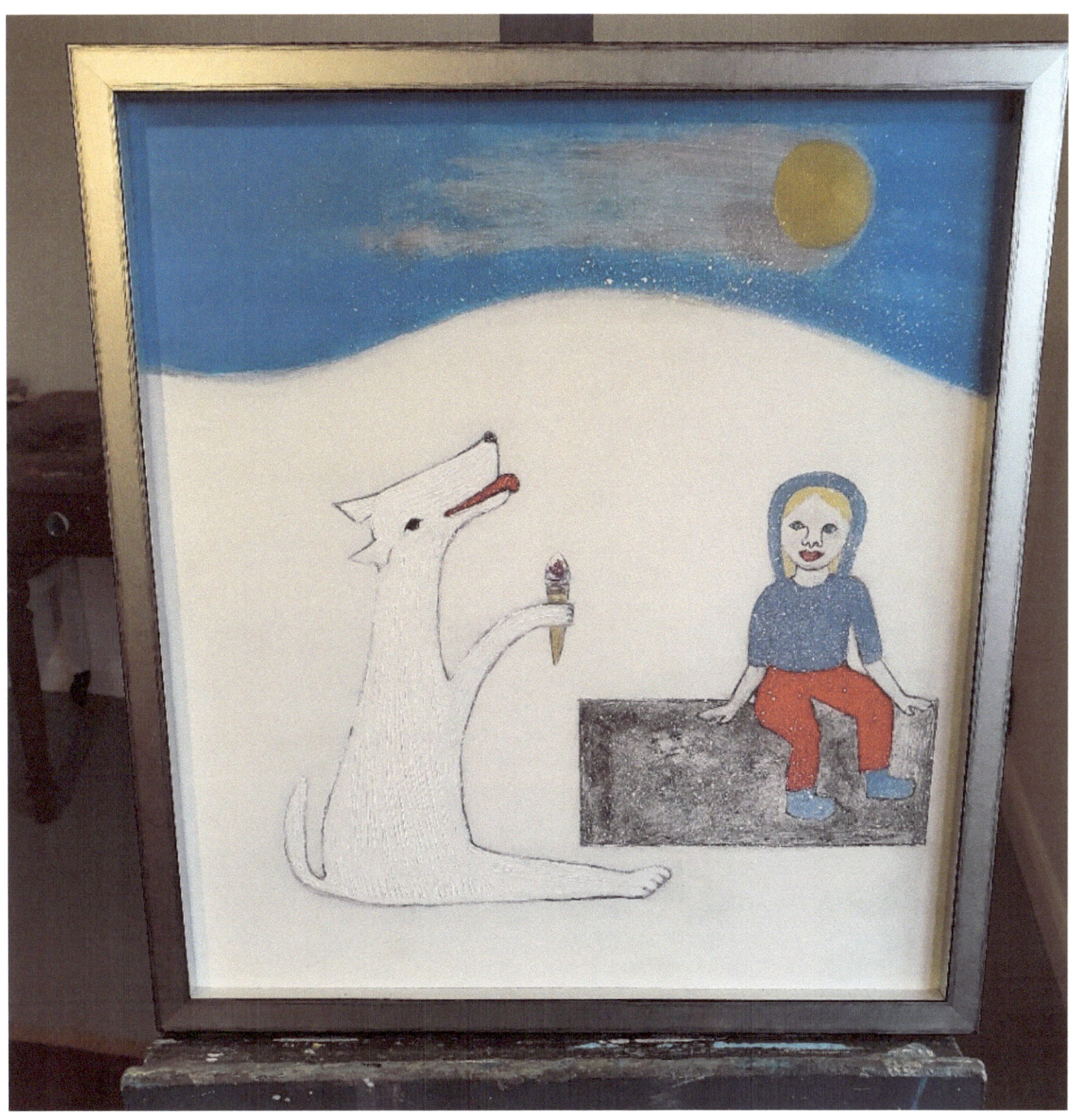

This symbolises gratitude and giving that which we love to others.

Thank you for reading this book, I do hope you have enjoyed it.

There will be more books in this series in time.

www.ingramcontent.com/pod-product-compliance
Lightning Source LLC
Chambersburg PA
CBHW060838290526
45792CB00006BB/1975